HISTC

MW01617288

in Their Places
A GUIDE TO WOMEN'S HISTORY SITES

MARCIA TREMMEL GOLDSTEIN

PHOTOGRAPHY BY
CAROLE D. CARDON

HISTORIC DENVER, INC.

This project was partially funded by a State Historical Fund grant award from the Colorado Historical Society, and with the assistance of Historic Denver, Inc. Historic Denver thanks the publication sponsor, the Autry Museum of Western Heritage, in celebration of its merger with the Women of the West Museum, for their generous support.

International Standard Book Number: 0-914248-34-0
Text copyright © 2002 Marcia Tremmel Goldstein
Photographs copyright © 2002 Carole D. Cardon unless otherwise noted.

Cover photo by Marcia Goldstein: Treat Hall, Colorado Women's College (1800 Pontiac Street)

Published by Historic Denver, Inc.
1536 Wynkoop Street, Suite 400A
Denver, Colorado 80202-1182

Sites marked **N®R** are listed in the National Register of Historic Places and those marked **D⊠L** have been designated Denver Landmarks.

Printed by Crossfire Graphics.

Editor: Lori D. Kranz
Proofreader: Susan Konarske
Indexer: Cyndie Chandler
Design and Composition: Cathy Calder, Blonde Ambition

CONTENTS

Acknowledgments 4
Introduction 6
The Tours
   Tour One: Whittier, Five Points, and Curtis Park. 8
   Tour Two: Park Hill and Capitol Hill 22
   Tour Three: Civic Center, Downtown, Lower Downtown,
      and Auraria 50
   Tour Four: Northwest Denver. 76
   Tour Five: South Denver. 86
Bibliography 98
Index 101

THIS LIMESTONE ROSE HONORS FLORENCE LAMONT'S SCHOOL OF MUSIC, FOUNDED IN 1924. THE NEWMAN CENTER FOR PERFORMING ARTS IS LOCATED ON THE UNIVERSITY OF DENVER CAMPUS (TOUR FIVE, STOP 2).
PHOTO BY MARCIA GOLDSTEIN

ACKNOWLEDGMENTS

When Kathleen Brooker and Kris Christensen of Historic Denver, Inc. proposed this guide to women's history sites, skeptics feared that the book would be too short. We hope we have proved the naysayers wrong. Our problem was not that we had too few sites, but too many! I wish to thank Kathleen and Kris for their perseverance, and the Colorado Historical Fund as well as the Autry Museum of Western Heritage for their generous underwriting of this project. We all present this guidebook as a starting point for diligent searchers to find many, many more *Denver Women in Their Places*.

My colleague Gail Beaton, a talented University of Colorado at Denver historian, compiled a great deal of research material for the sites, especially in Capitol Hill and downtown Denver. Photographer Carole Cardon searched out many hidden and far-flung sites. Lori Kranz's clever editing eased the pain and torture of cutting text. The book's remarkably talented and patient designer, Cathy Calder of Blonde Ambition, compiled our work while juggling a prolonged and tedious production

DENVER SALVATION ARMY WOMEN'S MARCHING BAND
PARADES DOWN 16TH STREET, CA. 1900.
PHOTO: DENVER PUBLIC LIBRARY, WESTERN HISTORY DEPARTMENT

schedule with her own wedding planning. The attractive and readable result of their efforts speaks for itself.

The idea for this guide originated with the Colorado Coalition for Women's History. CCWH president and historian Rebecca Hunt deserves much credit for supporting this project, as do CCWH board members: Gwen Scott, Joanne Emerson, Janet Cunningham, Linda Hoffman, Colleen Nunn, Becky Dorward, John Steinle, and Judge Larry Bohning.

Colleen Nunn, Bruce Hanson, and Coi Drummond Gehrig at the Denver Public Library Western History/Genealogy Department took a special interest in our efforts, as did the Colorado Historical Society library, and librarians Kathy Mitchell and Steve Fisher at the University of Denver Library Special Collections. Karen Miyagishima, Grace Stiles, Rebecca Hunt, Virginia Roberts Steele, Ann Student, Becky Dorward, and Jean Martine shared invaluable background material. Wallace Yvonne Tollette, director of the Black American West Museum and Heritage Center, reviewed sites in Five Points. The staff at Fairmount and Riverside Cemeteries provided vital statistics of deceased women who in life tried to hide their age. Many thanks to all!

My mother, Phyllis Tremmel, has taught me to treasure the resourcefulness of women. A talented former organ professor at Colorado Women's College, Phyllis has done more to preserve the history and campus of CWC than any other person. Jeff Goldstein, my loving husband who also loves all things high-tech, helped generate digital photo files for the book. The influence of Dr. Tom Noel, my lifelong mentor and generous friend, pervades every aspect of the research and writing of this book.

Last, I wish to remember Eleanor Gehres and Genevieve Fiore who were lifelong champions of women's history and women's rights in Denver. They are missed.

INTRODUCTION

Why do we need a guidebook for women's history sites in Denver? Because we've never had one! Our city's historical record has often neglected women. Early histories recorded the story of men, but overlooked early female Denverites. Cheyenne, Arapaho, and Ute women camped along Cherry Creek long before gold fever hit the Rocky Mountains. Female boardinghouse operators, prostitutes, and laundresses of all races, creeds, and colors filled the gold camps and town sites of Denver and Auraria in the 1850s and 1860s. Wives of wealthy "boosters" organized the first charities to curtail the unfortunate by-products of Denver's boom-and-bust mining economy: homelessness, poverty, and domestic violence. Working-class women sought living wages and more hours at home to raise their families. Women yearned for and built stability in the form of businesses, schools, churches, parks, and arts institutions. Savvy suffrage leaders in 1893 helped Denver women from all walks of life win the right to vote in Colorado. Throughout the twentieth century, Denver women have served in the state legislature and city government, and led many public institutions. Each year historians document more of our city's history of women, but there is still much left untold.

Women architects have come into their own only very recently, and this volume suffers greatly from the lack of historical sites designed by women. Men historically dominated the architectural and construction professions, and male owners and builders predominate in the property records of our landmarks. But the sites we have chosen are vivid reminders that philanthropic women like Mary Dean Reed, Margaret Tobin Brown, and Agnes Tammen often provided the vision and funds for the bricks and mortar of our public institutions. Professionals like Emily Griffith and Dr. Justina Ford ran schools and day care centers for the children of wage-earning women, or delivered health care and babies in the homes of poor families. Female domestic servants cleaned the mansions, laundry, and children of well-to-do philanthropists, who then had more time for good works. Men publicly led the city's churches, while nuns and churchwomen like Mothers Frances Cabrini and Mary Pancratia Bonfils actually

CHEYENNE, ARAPAHO, AND UTE WOMEN BUILT THE FIRST RESIDENTIAL DWELLINGS IN THE DENVER AREA. PHOTO: DENVER PUBLIC LIBRARY, WESTERN HISTORY DEPARTMENT

ran them. And Anne Evans, Dana Crawford, Ann Love, Geraldine Stepp, and Kathleen Brooker have led the movement for historic preservation in our city.

This short guidebook highlights the public lives of women and their organizations. Future guidebooks will, I hope, lead readers to more private places, where women engaged in the work of home management, domestic service, child-raising, food preparation, and decorative arts.

The tours are not intended as "walking tours," except for avid hikers. Take the bus, light rail, bicycle, or drive to destinations that may be miles apart. This guide will supplement other guidebooks and tours, providing the missing link to women's roles in our community's past. The fine books listed in the bibliography are all "must reads."

To the extent that women's history remains unpublished, we can say that women's story remains hidden from view. But the places where women have shaped history are visible monuments. This guide will help lead you to *Denver Women in Their Places*.

Marcia Tremmel Goldstein

TOUR ONE
WHITTIER, FIVE POINTS, AND CURTIS PARK

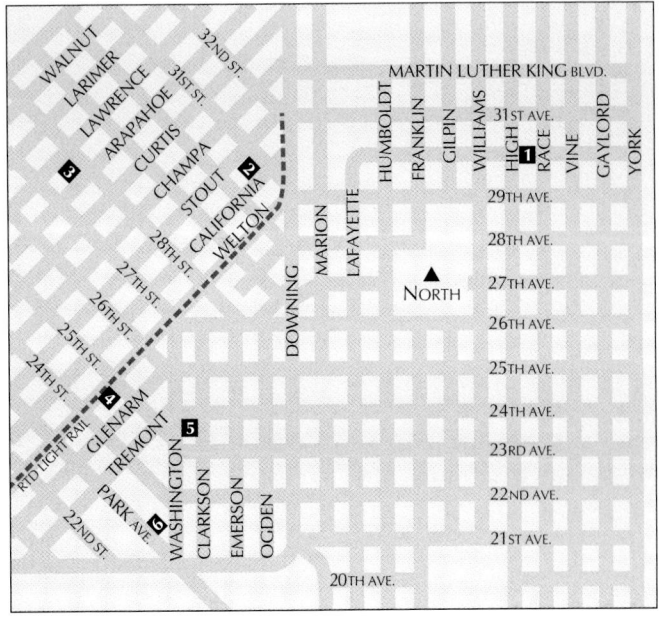

KEY

1. East 30th Ave. and High St. (Madam C. J. Walker Park)
2. 3091 California St. (Black American West Museum and Heritage Center/Dr. Justina Ford House)
3. 1128 28th St. (Margery Reed Mayo Day Nursery)
4. 2460 Welton St. (Phyllis Wheatley YWCA Branch)
5. 2357 Clarkson St. (George Washington Carver Day Nursery and Negro Women's Club Home)
6. 119 Park Ave. West (Shorter African Methodist Episcopal [A.M.E.] Church/Cleo Parker Robinson Dance School and Theater)

1 MADAM C. J. WALKER PARK
EAST 30TH AVENUE AND HIGH STREET

Denver's first city park named for an African-American woman was dedicated in May 2002. The park honors **Madam C. J. Walker** (1867–1919), the first self-made female millionaire in the United States. While living in Denver from 1905 to 1906, Walker founded Madam C. J. Walker Manufacturing Company, the world's leading distributor of African-American women's hair care products. Memorial panels at the quiet neighborhood park interpret Walker's life.

Born Sarah Breedlove in Louisiana in 1867, she married at age 14 and bore her daughter, A'Lelia, in 1885. Tired of working as a cook, maid, and washerwoman, Sarah perfected her own "Wonderful Hair Grower" in 1905, after moving to Denver. She began selling "Glossine" hair oil, "Temple Grower," and "Tetter Salve" to African-American women whose hair suffered from the city's dry climate. Sarah operated salons out of rooming houses at 2410 Champa Street and 2317 Lawrence Street in Denver's Five Points district.

In 1906, Sarah married newspaperman Charles Joseph Walker, and joined Shorter A.M.E. Church (see stop 6). Her daughter and future patron of the arts during the Harlem Renaissance, **A'Lelia Walker** (1885–1931), took over the Denver operation until it closed in 1907. Madam Walker, now divorced, traveled widely selling products, and in 1910 she established headquarters in Indianapolis. By 1917, Walker owned the largest black-owned business in the country, employing hundreds of black saleswomen. She donated generously to black colleges, the National Association for the Advancement of Colored People (NAACP), and black women's organizations.

Madam Walker died a millionaire at her Villa Lewaro estate in New York at age fifty-one in May 1919, leaving the business to A'Lelia. Her prestigious mansion in Irvington-on-Hudson, New York, and the Madam C. J. Walker building in Indianapolis are both designated National Historic Landmarks. The park renaming project was the brainchild of Grace Stiles, founder and director of the Stiles African-American Heritage Center in Five Points.

THIS NEIGHBORHOOD PARK WITH INTERPRETIVE PANELS IS DEDICATED TO
AMERICA'S FIRST WOMAN SELF-MADE MILLIONAIRE, MADAM C. J. WALKER,
WHO STARTED HER HAIR CARE PRODUCTS BUSINESS IN DENVER.
PHOTO BY MARCIA GOLDSTEIN

"I AM A WOMAN WHO CAME FROM THE COTTON FIELDS OF THE SOUTH.
I WAS PROMOTED FROM THERE TO THE WASHTUB. THEN I WAS PROMOTED
TO THE COOK KITCHEN, AND FROM THERE I PROMOTED MYSELF IN THE BUSINESS
OF MANUFACTURING HAIR GOODS AND PREPARATIONS . . . I HAVE BUILT MY OWN
FACTORY ON MY OWN GROUND." (MADAM C. J. WALKER, NATIONAL NEGRO
BUSINESS LEAGUE CONVENTION, 1912)

BLACK AMERICAN WEST MUSEUM AND HERITAGE CENTER/ DR. JUSTINA FORD HOUSE

3091 CALIFORNIA STREET

Architectural style: ITALIANATE
Built: 1890, 1988 (RENOVATION)
Architects: C. W. FENTRESS AND ASSOCIATES (RENOVATION)

The handsomely restored home of **Dr. Justina Warren Ford** (1871–1952), Denver's first black female physician, now houses the Black American West Museum and Heritage Center. The museum displays Dr. Ford's medical equipment and furnishings, as well as exhibits of African-American miners, cowboys, businesspeople, and soldiers who have lived in Colorado and the West.

Justina Warren was born in Knoxville, Illinois, in 1871, graduated from Hering Medical School in Chicago in 1899, then moved to Denver in 1902. Authorities reluctantly approved her medical license when Justina argued that thousands of Denver's immigrant and minority citizens needed her services. The "Lady Baby Doctor" made house calls by horse and buggy, taxi, then in her husband the Reverend Ford's automobile. She and many of her patients were often barred by race from public and private hospitals. By the end of World War II, Dr. Ford and her "black bag" had become a Five Points neighborhood fixture. Ford was finally admitted as a member of the American Medical Association the year of her death in 1952.

Dr. Ford's original Five Points home and office at 2335 Arapahoe Street escaped demolition when a group of Five Points neighbors, former patients, community leaders, museum founder Paul Stewart, and Historic Denver, Inc., halted the bulldozers and relocated the building to its present site in 1984. Project Director **Geraldine Stepp** oversaw the first preservation effort by a black organization in Colorado, in which more than 100 people from all walks of life saved this monument to "a magnificent humanitarian: a woman who stood tall and achieved in spite of the odds."

THE BLACK AMERICAN WEST MUSEUM
AND HERITAGE CENTER IS HOUSED IN
DR. FORD'S ORIGINAL TWO-STORY BRICK
HOME AND OFFICE, RELOCATED TO
ITS CURRENT SITE IN 1984.

DR. JUSTINA FORD, DENVER'S
FIRST BLACK WOMAN DOCTOR,
DELIVERED MORE THAN
7,000 BABIES OF EVERY
ETHNIC BACKGROUND.
PHOTO: DENVER PUBLIC LIBRARY,
WESTERN HISTORY DEPARTMENT

MARGERY REED MAYO DAY NURSERY

1128 28TH STREET

Architectural style: SPANISH REVIVAL

Built: 1926

Architect: HARRY JAMES MANNING

The Social Center and Day Nursery began caring for the children of working mothers who lived in the South Platte River slums known as the "bottoms" in 1898. Local charity women incorporated the day nursery in 1906.

One of Denver's most generous female benefactors, **Mary Dean (Mrs. Verner Z.) Reed** (1875–1945), took the nursery under her wing in 1915. Reed funded the construction of the attractive Spanish Revival, red brick and pink stucco facility at its current site in 1926, when the nursery took the name of the Reeds' beloved daughter, **Margery Reed Mayo** (1894–1925), who tragically died of illness.

Bessie Jack, the center's superintendent in the 1920s, claimed that "we don't herd children . . . there is no care like a mother's care—but we do try to be good substitutes." Each day the nursery cared for more than 85 babies, toddlers, and preschoolers of a rainbow of colors, religions, and ethnicities. Innovative Montessori kindergarten teachers instructed the children how to button shirts, tie shoes, and play tambourines. Tuition was 10 cents per day, but no child was turned away. The center offered job placement for mothers at local laundries, canneries, biscuit factories, and private homes.

By 1944 the Sisters of Charity of Cincinnati (who operated Sacred Heart School nearby) had taken over operation of the Mayo Day Nursery. After Mary Reed's death in 1945, *Denver Post* owner **Helen G. Bonfils** (1889–1972) donated a chapel in Reed's honor, along with a shrine of Our Lady of Guadalupe and a new "Tot's Lot" playground. The Mile High Child Care Association and Catholic Community Services still operate the century-old day-care center, for which they received Historic Denver, Inc.'s Community Preservation Award in 1998.

DENVER'S OLDEST
DAY CARE CENTER,
INCORPORATED IN 1906,
INHABITS THIS BRICK AND
STUCCO SPANISH REVIVAL
BUILDING DONATED BY
MARY DEAN REED
IN 1926.

CHILDREN OF ALL ETHNIC BACKGROUNDS HAVE PLAYED IN
THE "TOT'S LOT" PLAYGROUND SINCE THE 1940s.
PHOTO: DENVER PUBLIC LIBRARY, WESTERN HISTORY DEPARTMENT

4 PHYLLIS WHEATLEY YWCA BRANCH
2460 WELTON STREET (EXTINCT SITE)

Architectural style: QUEEN ANNE
Built: CA. 1887
Architect: UNKNOWN

A weedy vacant lot is all that remains of the Phyllis Wheatley Branch of the Young Women's Christian Association (YWCA), the principal social and recreation center for African-American women and girls in Denver for over five decades. Local black churchwomen founded Denver's "Phyllis Wheatley Colored YWCA Club" in 1916. Named after the eighteenth-century slave poet, the club reflected the YWCA's national pattern of racially segregated chapters.

During World War I, YWCA volunteers struggled to find housing and jobs for single black women in Denver, many of whom were new arrivals from the racially oppressive South. In 1920, Denver philanthropist **Mary Dean (Mrs. Verner Z.) Reed** (1875–1945) donated the handsome two-story brick former home of real estate developer William Barth at the corner of 25th and Welton Streets to house the YWCA branch's boarders and expanding programs.

During the 1920s and 1930s, the homey rooming house and social center attracted hundreds of young women, who joined the Business and Industrial Girls Club for adults, the Bon Amici Club and Girl Reserves for young girls and teenagers, the Young Married Club, and Camp Nizhoni, an all-black summer mountain camp at Lincoln Hills, Colorado. During World War II, the branch recruited women for war-industry jobs, and as hostesses for Denver's black USO.

From the 1940s to the 1960s, black and white YWCA women led protests to integrate Denver theaters, restaurants, and swimming pools. Branch chairwoman **Gertie N. Ross** (1879–1961) was the first black member of the Central YWCA Board, which eventually desegregated YWCA facilities citywide. In 1964 the Denver YWCA dismantled the Phyllis Wheatley Branch to comply with local and national racial integration policies, and the building was soon sold and razed.

(ABOVE) THIS HANDSOME QUEEN ANNE, FORMER HOME OF FIVE POINTS
DEVELOPER WILLIAM BARTH, BECAME THE PHYLLIS WHEATLEY BRANCH YWCA
IN 1920. IN 1964 THE BRANCH DISBANDED AND THE BUILDING
WAS SOLD AND RAZED. (BELOW) THE "GIRL RESERVES" AND OTHER YWCA
CLUBS GATHERED AT THE "Y" TO SOCIALIZE AND RECREATE IN THE 1940s.

PHOTOS: COLORADO HISTORICAL SOCIETY

5 GEORGE WASHINGTON CARVER DAY NURSERY AND NEGRO WOMEN'S CLUB HOME
2357 CLARKSON STREET

Architectural style: ITALIANATE
Built: 1894
Architect: UNKNOWN

Denver's oldest African-American day-care center opened in 1917 as the Negro Women's Club Association Day Nursery in this two-story brick residence in Denver's Five Points neighborhood. Local black women's clubs led by **Ida DePriest** (ca. 1862–1931) and **Gertie N. Ross** (1879–1961) established a working women's residence and clubhouse, in keeping with the motto of the National Association of Negro Women's Clubs, "Lifting as We Climb." The center soon took in children for day care, enabling black working women, who were restricted by racial codes to the lowest-paying jobs, to make ends meet. For decades the day nursery has offered free or low-cost day care, as well as peace of mind for Denver mothers.

The original facility accommodated up to fifty children ages two through twelve. In addition to a hearty hot lunch, preschoolers enjoyed a morning snack supplemented by cod liver oil in the winter. Physicians visited the nursery regularly for health inspections. In good weather, children escaped the crowded classrooms into a small playground in back.

In 1945 the Community Chest took over the funding of the nursery, but left the operations to members of Denver's black women's clubs, including the Self Improvement and Social Service Club, the Taka Club, the Carnation Club, and the Pond Lily Art and Literary Club. The nursery took the name George Washington Carver Day Nursery in 1948, after the great African-American scientist. In 1966 the center moved to new quarters a few blocks east at 2260 Humboldt Street. The Mile High Child Care Association operates Carver Day Nursery at the newer site, offering day care on a sliding fee scale. The original building has since been restored as a private residence.

THIS PAINTED BRICK ITALIANATE 1890S HOME WITH ORNATE WOOD BRACKETS HOUSED THE GEORGE WASHINGTON CARVER DAY NURSERY FROM 1917 TO 1966. NOTE THE INVITING FIRE ESCAPE SLIDE.

BLACK WOMEN'S CLUBS SPONSORED THE HOMEY, LOW-COST DAY-CARE CENTER, WHERE FIFTY CHILDREN ATE TASTY SNACKS AND NAPPED EACH DAY WHILE MOTHERS WORKED.

PHOTOS: DENVER PUBLIC LIBRARY, WESTERN HISTORY DEPARTMENT

SHORTER AFRICAN METHODIST EPISCOPAL (A.M.E.) CHURCH/ CLEO PARKER ROBINSON DANCE SCHOOL AND THEATER

119 PARK AVENUE WEST

Architectural style: SPANISH MISSION

Built: 1888, 1926

Architects: IRELAND AND PARR

Black pioneers **Mary E. Smith** and **Mary Randolph** (d. 1901) raised money from faro and poker players on Holiday Street (now Market Street), then founded Denver's first "Colored" A.M.E. church in 1866. Parishioners built a grand Gothic Revival structure at the current Park Avenue site in 1888, where the founding leaders of many of Denver's first African-American women's organizations worshiped. Community activist **Gertie N. Ross** (1879–1961) served as Shorter's church organist for more than fifty years. A tragic fire, probably set by the Ku Klux Klan, destroyed the church in 1925. Within one year, African-American architects and builders erected a handsome new Spanish Mission–style church, which flourished for the next fifty years. Since 1990, the Shorter congregation has gathered at a modern parish complex located at 3100 Richard Allen Court.

Cleo Parker Robinson (1948–), a graduate of Denver Public Schools and Colorado Women's College, formed her first dance ensemble in 1970 as part of a Model Cities federal antipoverty program. She combined modern dance, ballet, and African dance roots to create a new improvisational performance style.

An audience of 300 patrons now enjoys African and modern dance performances in the former sanctuary, and dance students attend classes in former Sunday school rooms at Robinson's headquarters and studios at the historic Shorter Church. The popular company performs at hundreds of schools, community centers, and concert halls in the U.S., Africa, and worldwide.

BLACK ARCHITECTS AND BUILDERS ERECTED THIS HANDSOME, ASYMMETRICAL,
BLOND-BRICK, SPANISH MISSION–STYLE CHURCH IN 1926 AFTER THE KU KLUX
KLAN ALLEGEDLY BURNED THE 1888 SHORTER A.M.E. CHURCH BUILDING.

WORLD-CLASS DANCE ARTIST
CLEO PARKER ROBINSON HAS
RECYCLED THE HISTORIC
SHORTER CHURCH INTO
DANCE STUDIOS AND A THEATER.

PHOTO BY KERMIT HAYES,
COURTESY OF CLEO PARKER ROBINSON DANCE

TOUR TWO
PARK HILL AND CAPITOL HILL

21ST AVE.

MONTVIEW BLVD.

19TH AVE.

1

18TH AVE.

17TH AVE.

NIAGARA
NEWPORT
ONEIDA
OLIVE
PONTIAC
POPLAR
QUEBEC

COLFAX AVE.

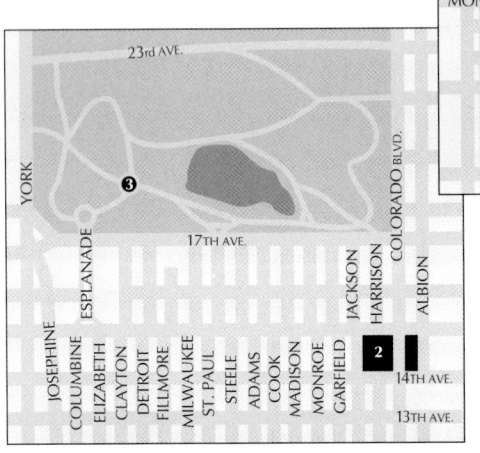

23rd AVE.

YORK

ESPLANADE

3

17TH AVE.

JOSEPHINE
COLUMBINE
ELIZABETH
CLAYTON
DETROIT
FILLMORE
MILWAUKEE
ST. PAUL
STEELE
ADAMS
COOK
MADISON
MONROE
GARFIELD
JACKSON
HARRISON
COLORADO BLVD.
ALBION

2

14TH AVE.

13TH AVE.

▲
NORTH

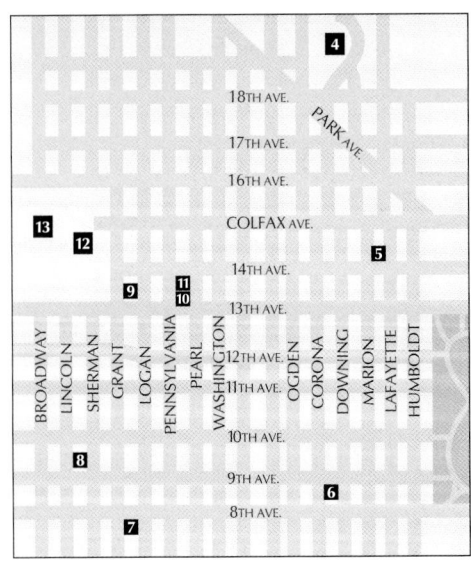

4

18TH AVE.

17TH AVE.

PARK AVE.

16TH AVE.

13

12

COLFAX AVE.

14TH AVE.

5

9

11
10

13TH AVE.

BROADWAY
LINCOLN
SHERMAN
GRANT
LOGAN
PENNSYLVANIA
PEARL
WASHINGTON

12TH AVE.
11TH AVE.
10TH AVE.

OGDEN
CORONA
DOWNING
MARION
LAFAYETTE
HUMBOLDT

8

9TH AVE.

6

8TH AVE.

7

KEY

1. East 17th to East 21st Aves., Oneida to Quebec Sts. (Colorado Women's College/ Johnson & Wales University)
2. 1400 Jackson St. (National Jewish Medical and Research Center)
3. Denver City Park (Martin Luther King, Jr. Monument)
4. 1056 East 19th Ave. (Children's Hospital/Agnes Reid Tammen Hall)
5. 1410 Marion St. (Wolcott School/Wolcott Arms Apartments)
6. 846 Corona St. (Dora Moore School)
7. 400 East 8th Ave. (Colorado Governor's Residence/Cheesman-Evans-Boettcher Mansion)
8. 940 Lincoln St. (Woman's Club of Denver)
9. 1325 Logan St. (Denver Woman's Press Club)
10. 1340 Pennsylvania St. (Molly Brown House Museum)
11. 1370 Pennsylvania St. (St. Mary's Academy/ Salvation Army Building)
12. 200 East Colfax Ave. (Colorado State Capitol)
13. East Colfax Ave. and Broadway (Sadie Likens Monument)

COLORADO WOMEN'S COLLEGE/ JOHNSON & WALES UNIVERSITY
EAST 17TH TO EAST 21ST AVENUES, ONEIDA TO QUEBEC STREETS

TREAT HALL (1800 PONTIAC STREET)   **NⓇR DⓁL**
Architectural style: RICHARDSONIAN ROMANESQUE
Built: 1889–1909, 1916 (BRICK ADDITION) Architect: FRANK H. JACKSON

FOOTE HALL (7150 MONTVIEW BOULEVARD)
Architectural style: TUDOR GOTHIC
Built: 1929 Architect: S. ARTHUR AXTENS

WHATLEY CHAPEL (1800 ONEIDA STREET)
Architectural style: MODERN GOTHIC
Built: 1962 Architect: STANLEY MORSE

Colorado Women's College was often called the "Vassar of the West" from 1909 until it closed its doors in 1982. A dedicated core of Baptists founded CWC in 1886, dreaming of a Protestant nondenominational college dedicated to higher learning for women. They laid the foundation for Treat Hall in 1889, but could not complete the four-story sandstone and granite structure until almost twenty-five years later.

Martha (Mrs. F. I.) Smith (d. 1944) organized the Baptist Women's Auxiliary in the early 1890s, who launched a fund-raising campaign for the college with the crusading zeal of suffragists. They staged a dramatic "March of Women" along East Colfax Avenue to the CWC campus in 1902, and raised over $35,000. The women also gathered linens, tables, and desks for dorm rooms when Treat Hall, named later for the college's first president, finally opened its doors to students in 1909. Martha Smith served as the first woman on the board of trustees, which elected her as its only woman president in 1932.

The early CWC curriculum combined liberal arts courses with the "Upper and Lower Home Arts," including "Rational Living," "Domestic Science and Efficiency," "Home Decorating," and "Fundamentals of Child Life." Teacher salaries were $50–$75 per month. For diversion, students

THE RUSTICATED,
GRAY GRANITE AND
RED SANDSTONE
TREAT HALL IS
DOMINATED BY ITS
1916 BRICK ADDITON.
PHOTO BY MARCIA GOLDSTEIN

THE COLLEGE'S
INAUGURAL 1909
FRESHMAN CLASS PLAYS
A MEAN CROQUET GAME
ON THE GROUNDS OF
THEIR DORMITORY AND
CLASSROOM BUILDING,
TREAT HALL.
PHOTO: SPECIAL COLLECTIONS
DEPARTMENT, PENROSE LIBRARY,
UNIVERSITY OF DENVER,
CWC COLLECTION

organized a basketball team, which competed in sporty green and white bloomer uniforms.

The trustees added a brick expansion wing to Treat Hall in 1916. An attractive Tudor Gothic–style dormitory, named Foote Hall for its chief benefactor, **Retta Ann Foote** (1861–1959), was completed in 1929. Foote's son and daughter-in-law, Don and **Margaret Sharpless Foote** (1895–1994), donated the magnificent 3,000-pipe Retta Foote Memorial Organ in 1962 as the centerpiece of Whatley Chapel. This stately ecumenical house of worship, named for benefactors Barney and **Gertrude Whatley** (1889–1974), was built in 1962 and designed by architect Stanley Morse. Inside, thirty-nine stained-glass windows by the French artist Gabriel Loire feature historic leaders, including Hull House founder, social worker, and peace activist **Jane Addams** (1860–1935).

Colorado Women's College expanded for seven decades, offering academic and leadership opportunities to women rarely available at male-dominated coeducational institutions. With the rise of feminism in the 1970s, segregated women's education grew out of favor. This trend combined with severe financial troubles to force the closure of CWC in 1982.

When the University of Denver (DU) purchased the defunct CWC campus in 1982, university officials built the Lowell Thomas Law Building in 1984 and relocated the Lamont School of Music (Tour Five, stop 2) to CWC's former Houston Fine Arts Center. During its tenure at the Park Hill campus, DU founded its innovative Women's College, which offers college courses and degrees for working women on weekends and evenings. The Women's College now operates from the Mary Reed Building on DU's University Park Campus (Tour Five, stop 2). An enthusiastic Colorado Women's College Alumni Association also keeps the CWC legacy alive.

Johnson & Wales (J&W) University began purchasing the historic CWC campus in 1999. J&W is a multicampus, international business and hospitality college founded by **Gertrude I. Johnson** (1876–1961) and **Mary T. Wales** (1874–1952) in 1914 in Providence, Rhode Island. Portraits of Miss Johnson and Miss Wales greet visitors to the handsomely restored, oak-trimmed Foote Hall, which serves as the school's administrative offices. J&W University's ambitious plans include a long-overdue restoration of historic Treat Hall as a student-run bed-and-breakfast inn.

FOOTE HALL, A 1929 BLOND-BRICK AND TERRA-COTTA TUDOR-STYLE DORMITORY, HAS BEEN RESTORED BY JOHNSON & WALES UNIVERSITY.

WHATLEY CHAPEL AND ITS COMPANION TOWER, WHICH HOUSES THE THIRTY-BELL HILL CARILLON.

NATIONAL JEWISH MEDICAL AND RESEARCH CENTER
1400 JACKSON STREET

BEAUMONT NURSES' HOME
Architectural style: COLONIAL REVIVAL
Built: 1922 Architect: T. ROBERT WIEGER

B'NAI B'RITH BUILDING
(SOUTHEAST CORNER OF COLFAX AVENUE AND COLORADO BOULEVARD)
Architectural style: RENAISSANCE REVIVAL
Built: 1926 Architects: FISHER AND FISHER, MOUNTJOY AND FREWAN

Jewish women worked tirelessly to alleviate poverty and disease among late nineteenth-century indigent health-seekers attracted by Denver's dry, sunny climate. National Jewish Hospital (NJH), founded in 1892 and now the "Global Leader in Research and Treatment of Lung, Allergic and Immune Diseases," is a monument to their efforts.

Frances Wisebart Jacobs (1843–1892) distributed food and medicines in Denver's slums, and organized the nondenominational Charity Organization Society in 1887, the forerunner of today's United Way. Her dream of a hospital for lung disease victims materialized when ground broke for the Frances Jacobs Hospital in 1892, just months after her tragic death from illness. The hospital opened in 1899 at Jackson Street and East Colfax Avenue.

Russian-born **Fannie Eller Lorber** (1881–1958) founded the Denver Sheltering Home for Jewish Children in 1907 to house indigent orphans. Lorber's nationwide fund-raising network spurred expansion into a children's treatment center. In 1978, the renamed National Asthma Center merged with NJH.

Seraphine Eppstein Pisko (1861–1942) served NJH for over forty years as a formidable board member, executive secretary, and vice president. Pisko oversaw dramatic expansion of NJH into a 16.5-acre campus, including the Beaumont Nurses' Home (the oldest surviving structure), a Women's Pavilion named for her in 1925 (no longer standing), and the massive B'nai B'rith Children's Infirmary Building.

THE MASSIVE FOUR-STORY RENAISSANCE REVIVAL B'NAI B'RITH BUILDING STILL BEARS THE HOSPITAL'S ORIGINAL MOTTO: "NONE MAY ENTER WHO CAN PAY, NONE CAN PAY WHO ENTER." PHOTO BY MARCIA GOLDSTEIN

DENVER'S "MOTHER OF CHARITIES," FRANCES WISEBART JACOBS, HELPED FOUND NATIONAL JEWISH HOSPITAL IN 1892.
PHOTO: REPRESENTATIVE WOMEN OF COLORADO

3 MARTIN LUTHER KING, JR. MONUMENT
DENVER CITY PARK—WEST OF CITY PARK PAVILION, ONE BLOCK NORTH OF 17TH AVENUE

Built: 2002
Sculptor: ED DWIGHT

An imposing bronze statue of civil rights leader and Nobel Peace Prize winner Dr. Martin Luther King, Jr. (1929–1968), towers 25 feet high over City Park, atop the city's newest and finest granite monument. On a second tier stand life-sized statues of four of history's most significant humanitarians and civil rights leaders: abolitionist and women's rights orator **Sojourner Truth** (ca. 1797–1883); the "mother" of the modern civil rights movement, **Rosa McCauley Parks** (1913–); Indian pacifist Mahatma Gandhi (1869–1948); and abolitionist and suffragist Frederick Douglass (1818–1895). On the ground level, Denver artist Ed Dwight's bas-reliefs and inscriptions of King's words depict African-American history.

The $1.3 million monument was dedicated in June 2002 by Mayor Wellington Webb and First Lady **Wilma J. Webb** (1943–). As a state legislator, Wilma Webb led the struggle from 1973 to 1984 to win designation of King's birthday as a state holiday. Webb's ongoing efforts to commemorate the King holiday have made Denver's celebration each January one of the largest in the country.

"I HAVE A DREAM THAT ONE DAY THIS NATION WILL RISE UP AND LIVE THE TRUE MEANING OF ITS CREED."
—MARTIN LUTHER KING, JR., AUGUST 1963

ABOLITIONIST SOJOURNER TRUTH, RIGHT, AND MONTGOMERY BUS BOYCOTT ORGANIZER ROSA PARKS, CENTER, ARE MEMORIALIZED IN SCULPTOR ED DWIGHT'S GRAND MONUMENT TO MARTIN LUTHER KING, JR., IN CITY PARK.

PHOTO BY MARCIA GOLDSTEIN

4 CHILDREN'S HOSPITAL
AGNES REID TAMMEN HALL
1056 EAST 19TH AVENUE
Architectural style: ART DECO
Built: 1917–1921
Architects: M. H. & B. HOYT ARCHITECTS

Women dominated Children's Hospital during its founding decades, when society considered women to be "naturally" suited to the care of children. The hospital's founding "mover and shaker" was **Dr. Minnie C. T. Love** (1855–1942). Minnehaha Cecelia Francesca Tucker earned her medical degree at Howard University, one of the few medical schools to accept women in the nineteenth century. After she and her husband, Charles C. Love, moved to Denver, Dr. Love opened the "Baby's Summer Hospital" in 1897. For two summers, Love and six nurses treated fifty children in two rows of tattered canvas tents at East 18th Avenue and Gaylord Street.

Belle Barton (Mrs. Frederick G.) Bonfils (d. 1935) and **Agnes Reid (Mrs. Harry H.) Tammen** (1865–1942), the influential wives of the *Denver Post*'s owners, formed the Children's Hospital Association in 1907. They opened a permanent hospital in 1910 at 2221 Downing Street, the former site of the Denver Maternity and Women's Hospital.

Oca Rush Cushman (1869–1962) served as the hospital's super-intendent for forty-five years until her retirement in 1955. A graduate of St. Luke's Hospital School of Nursing, Cushman ruled the hospital with a white-gloved iron hand, roaming the halls searching for dirt, mending uniforms, testing meals, and prodding indolent nurses. The hospital's nursing school graduated more than 500 pediatric nurses before it closed in 1956.

Children's Hospital expanded into facilities at the hospital's current Downing Street site in 1917. The Agnes Reid Tammen Hall, a handsome blond-brick Art Deco building still in use, was dedicated in 1921. The continuously expanding Children's Hospital complex will eventually relocate into new twenty-first-century facilities at the former Fitzsimons Medical Center site in Aurora.

A KEYSTONE SCULPTURE OF A GLEEFUL
CHILD AND TILES OF TOYS AND FLOWERS
FRAME THE ORIGINAL ENTRANCE TO
CHILDREN'S HOSPITAL.

PEDIATRIC NURSES GATHER AT FEEDING TIME FOR INFANTS
AND TODDLERS, CA. 1925.

PHOTOS: DENVER PUBLIC LIBRARY, WESTERN HISTORY DEPARTMENT

5 WOLCOTT SCHOOL/ WOLCOTT ARMS APARTMENTS

1410 MARION STREET
Architectural style: RENAISSANCE REVIVAL
Built: 1896 Architect: FREDERICK J. STERNER

Anna Wolcott Vaile (1868–1928) founded Wolcott School for Girls in 1898 as a private "finishing school" for the daughters of Denver's rich and famous. The complex included state-of-the-art classrooms, dormitories, gymnasiums, and a grand auditorium. The painted brick landmark, now apartments, is distinctive for its rows of balconies and arched windows.

Wolcott began in 1892 as principal of Wolfe Hall, an Episcopal girls' academy at 1300 Clarkson Street. In 1898 she founded Wolcott School and directed it for over twenty-five years until her retirement in 1924. Admirers described her as a tall, dignified woman of grace, manners, and intelligence, famous for her mauve-colored electric car.

6 DORA MOORE SCHOOL

846 CORONA STREET
Architectural style: ROMANESQUE REVIVAL
Built: 1889, 1993 (RESTORATION)
Architects: ROBERT S. ROESCHLAUB, STANLEY POUW ASSOC. (RESTORATION)

Denver Public Schools' oldest and finest school landmark began as Corona School in 1889, then took the name of its beloved principal, **Dora Moore** (1855–1938), the year of her death. Robert Roeschlaub, Denver's premier school architect, designed the massive brick and red sandstone structure. Students, parents, teachers, and alumni saved the landmark and its 1909 addition from demolition in the late 1970s. The school enjoyed a handsome restoration in 1993.

Dora Moore taught at Corona School from 1892 to 1929, and walked to school from her home at 1031 Emerson Street. Noteworthy women who attended Moore include former First Lady **Mamie Doud Eisenhower** (1896–1979) and folksinger and recording artist **Judy Collins** (1939–).

WOLCOTT SCHOOL STUDENTS GATHER AT THE
SCHOOL BUILDING NEAR CHEESEMAN PARK FOR AN
AUTO TOUR OF DENVER AROUND 1913.
PHOTO: DENVER PUBLIC LIBRARY, WESTERN HISTORY DEPARTMENT

BELL-SHAPED DOMES
ATOP FOUR ARCHED
STONE AND
TERRA-COTTA
ENTRYWAYS
DISTINGUISH
DORA MOORE
SCHOOL, THE
FIRST PUBLIC
SCHOOL LANDMARKED
BY DENVER.
PHOTO BY TOM NOEL

COLORADO GOVERNOR'S RESIDENCE/CHEESMAN-EVANS-BOETTCHER MANSION

400 EAST 8TH AVENUE

Architectural style: GEORGIAN REVIVAL
Built: 1908, 1980s (RESTORATION)
Architects: WILLIS A. MAREAN AND ALBERT J. NORTON, EDWARD D. WHITE, JR. (RESTORATION)

Denver's controversial real estate magnate and Water Department founder Walter Scott Cheesman never lived in this magnificent blood-red brick mansion. His widow, **Alice Foster Cheesman** (d. 1923), and daughter, **Gladys Cheesman Evans** (1887–1974), built the stately 24,000-square-foot, twenty-seven-room edifice after his death in 1907. The Cheesman women also donated the white marble Cheesman Park Memorial Pavilion in his honor. Claude and **Edna Case Boettcher** (d. 1958) purchased the lavish home in 1923, and the Boettcher family donated it to the people of Colorado as the governor's residence in 1958. Governor Steve and First Lady **Marjory McNichols** became official "first residents" in 1960.

The First Ladies who have resided here have offered extensive public access to the mansion. Historic preservationist **Ann Daniels (Mrs. John A.) Love** (1914–1999) organized the first public tours while raising her daughter, who would become State Supreme Court Justice **Rebecca Love Courlis** (1952–). "I learned to keep everything purse-size put away whenever we had big crowds," Ann recalled. KOA radio personality **Merrie Lynn (Mrs. John) Vanderhoof** brought an artists' series, concerts, and lectures. Former candidate for U.S. Senate **Dottie Venard (Mrs. Richard) Lamm** (1937–) worked ten hours a day as First Lady, and wrote a column on women's issues for the *Denver Post*. Education advocate **Bea (Mrs. Roy) Romer** oversaw a major exterior restoration in the 1980s. Suburbanites Bill and **Frances Owens** do not reside in the mansion; however, Frances redecorated the interior in 2001, with new furnishings, stylish color schemes, and inviting rearrangements of the rooms.

For more information, see *Geology Tour of Denver's Capitol Hill Stone Buildings*.

THE STATELY GEORGIAN REVIVAL GOVERNOR'S RESIDENCE, THE FORMER HOME OF
THE CHEESMAN AND BOETTCHER FAMILIES, BOASTS MASSIVE WHITE IONIC
COLUMNS THAT EXTEND FROM WOODEN DENTILED CORNICES.

A PORTRAIT GALLERY OF COLORADO'S FIRST LADIES,
ORIGINALLY ASSEMBLED BY ANN LOVE, GRACES THE
BARROOM ON THE FIRST FLOOR.

PHOTO BY MARCIA GOLDSTEIN

WOMAN'S CLUB OF DENVER
940 LINCOLN STREET

Architectural style: MODERN
Built: 1960
Architect: UNKNOWN

The Woman's Club of Denver (WCD), founded by educated upper-middle-class women in 1894, agitated for hundreds of social, political, and legal reforms. Early meetings took place at Unity Church at 19th and Broadway until the group erected a three-story brick clubhouse at 1347 Glenarm Place in 1902. The WCD moved in 1960 to modern facilities at 940 Lincoln Street (still in use today as a private event center). Membership declines forced the WCD to disband in the early 1990s.

Club founders **Sarah Platt Decker** (1852–1912) (Tour Five, stop 3), **Dr. Mary Barker Bates** (1823–1924), and **Ella Strong Denison** (1855–1940) emulated the Chicago Women's Club, which formed departments such as philanthropy, legislation, art, literature, and education. Members gathered to hear nationally known lecturers, learn public speaking, and hone organizational and business skills. WCD members formed the backbone of the Denver and State Federation of Women's Clubs, powerful networks of hundreds of women's clubs. Sarah Platt Decker gained acclaim as president of the General Federation of Women's Clubs from 1904 to 1908.

The WCD sponsored traveling libraries, free clinics and dispensaries, day nurseries, homeless shelters, and adult education classes. The nonpartisan club also successfully lobbied for an eight-hour-workday law for women, pure food laws, a state employment bureau, Mesa Verde and Rocky Mountain National Parks, electoral reform, the State Home for Dependent Children, mothers' pensions (welfare benefits), and Judge Ben Lindsey's innovative Juvenile Court.

THE MODERNISTIC 1960 WOMAN'S CLUB OF
DENVER FACILITY (BOTTOM) REPLACED THE HISTORIC
THREE-STORY BRICK CLUBHOUSE, BUILT IN 1902
AT 1347 GLENARM PLACE (TOP).

PHOTO: (TOP) DENVER PUBLIC LIBRARY,
WESTERN HISTORY DEPARTMENT

DENVER WOMAN'S PRESS CLUB   N■R D■L
1325 LOGAN STREET

Architectural style: ENGLISH COTTAGE
Built: 1910
Architects: VARIAN AND VARIAN

Journalist and suffragist **Minnie J. Reynolds** (1865–1936) formed the Denver Woman's Press Club (DWPC) in 1898 with nineteen other notable female journalists. The club reflected the growing influence of early twentieth-century newspaperwomen despite male domination of the profession. The DWPC's founders hoped "to advance and encourage women in literary work, to cultivate acquaintance and friendship among women of literary tastes, to secure the benefits arising from organized effort," and most importantly, "to drive dull care away."

M. J. Reynolds's first Denver assignment was as society editor for the *Rocky Mountain News*. In a long black skirt, starched white blouse, and feathered hat, Minnie bicycled from mansion to mansion in Capitol Hill reporting the latest gossip. A feminist at heart, Reynolds served as press secretary for the Colorado Equal Suffrage Association during its successful 1893 campaign, winning over 75 percent of the state's newspaper editors to support women's right to vote. National suffrage leaders recruited her to work on the East Coast for the Susan B. Anthony (Nineteenth) Amendment until its passage in 1920.

As the "mother" of the Denver Woman's Press Club, Minnie helped purchase its historic clubhouse for $9,000 from Denver artist George Elbert Burr in 1924. Burr built the small, purplish red brick cottage and studio in 1910, which the Press Club converted to meeting rooms, kitchen facilities, and archival offices. The club meets regularly in the inviting interior, including the large two-story studio with vaulted ceiling and skylights. The club, which boasts over 200 members, commemorated its centennial year in 1998 and published a book on its remarkable history.

For more information, see *Molly Brown's Capitol Hill Neighborhood*.

DENVER WOMAN'S PRESS CLUB FOUNDER AND SUFFRAGIST
MINNIE J. REYNOLDS AT HER DESK. Photo: Denver Woman's Press Club

ARTIST GEORGE BURR'S BRICK COTTAGE WAS CONVERTED TO THE DENVER
WOMAN'S PRESS CLUB HOUSE IN 1924. FOUNDED IN 1898, THE CLUB IS
ONE OF DENVER'S OLDEST SURVIVING AND THRIVING WOMEN'S ASSOCIATIONS.
PHOTO BY MARCIA GOLDSTEIN

MOLLY BROWN HOUSE MUSEUM

NR DL

1340 PENNSYLVANIA STREET

Architectural style: QUEEN ANNE WITH RICHARDSONIAN ROMANESQUE ELEMENTS

Built: **1889** Architect: WILLIAM LANG

The historic home of "The Unsinkable" **Margaret Tobin Brown** (1867–1932) is a popular tourist attraction. Brown's remarkable survival of the sunken ship *Titanic* has inspired Broadway musicals, Hollywood movies, romanticized books, and her fictional name, "Molly." A 1970 campaign to save the pink and gray rhyolite mansion with red sandstone trim from demolition spurred the formation of Historic Denver, Inc., which operates the house museum today.

Margaret Tobin, a spirited young Irish woman from Missouri, moved to the mining boomtown of Leadville, Colorado, in 1886. She married Irish-American prospector J. J. Brown, and the couple soon struck gold. In 1893, the Browns paid cash for a showy Queen Anne mansion designed by the city's premier architect, William Lang, in the heart of Capitol Hill. Margaret Brown decorated the interior with lavish, exotic furnishings inspired by her world travels.

In 1912, Brown survived the ill-fated voyage of the *Titanic*, courageously assisted women and children aboard lifeboats, and personally intervened to win compensation for the families of *Titanic* victims, survivors, and employees. She ran for the U.S. Senate on the National Woman's Party ticket in 1914. She helped striking coal miners' families during the 1914 Ludlow massacre, after the National Guard burned a union tent camp, killing fourteen women and children. She donated generously to Catholic institutions and supported Judge Ben Lindsey's Juvenile Court.

The Browns lived largely separate lives until J. J.'s death in 1922. Upon Margaret's death in 1932, the once lavish mansion served as a group home for troubled girls. The building languished until Colorado's First Lady, **Ann Daniels (Mrs. John A.) Love** (1914–1999), and Historic Denver, Inc., restored the historic home in 1970.

For more information, see *Molly Brown's Capitol Hill Neighborhood* and *Geology Tour of Denver's Capitol Hill Stone Buildings*.

Titanic survivor Margaret Brown was a women's rights activist, savvy politician, and generous philanthropist.

Margaret Tobin Brown's elegant 1890 stone mansion lives on as Denver's premier house museum.

11 ST. MARY'S ACADEMY/SALVATION ARMY BUILDING

1370 PENNSYLVANIA STREET

Architectural style: NEOCLASSICAL
Built: 1911 Architect: UNKNOWN

Margaret "Molly" Tobin Brown (1867–1932) (stop 10) was instrumental in bringing Denver's oldest Catholic girls' school from downtown into her Capitol Hill neighborhood in 1911. By then, St. Mary's Academy was steeped in almost fifty years of history. At the behest of Bishop Joseph Projectus Machebeuf, Sisters of Loretto **Beatrice Maes**, **Ignatia Mora**, and **Joanna Walsh** of Santa Fe founded St. Mary's in 1864 as Colorado's first private academy for girls. By the 1880s, nineteen teaching nuns and their forty young charges crowded into catechism classes at 15th and California Streets. **Mother Mary Pancratia Bonfils** (1852–1915), also the founding mother of Loretto Heights College (Tour Five, stop 5), established a larger school building at the same downtown site in 1882.

When the ambitious Mother Bonfils decided to further expand St. Mary's, she called on Margaret Tobin Brown, one of her "angels," for financial help. A massive neoclassical red brick structure soon filled the block at East 14th Avenue and Pennsylvania Street, where thousands of Catholic school girls attended classes from 1911 to 1951.

St. Mary's Academy relocated to modern facilities on South University Boulevard in Cherry Hills in 1951, where the campus thrives today. The historic St. Mary's building housed F. W. Woolworth office workers until 1968, then secretarial students at Parks School of Business until 1976. The current occupant is the Salvation Army, a century-old Denver charity.

For more information, see *Molly Brown's Capitol Hill Neighborhood*.

FROM 1911 TO 1951, THIS RED BRICK NEOCLASSICAL
CAPITOL HILL LANDMARK HOUSED DENVER'S OLDEST
CATHOLIC GIRLS' SCHOOL, FOUNDED IN 1864.

YOUNG GIRLS AND BOYS (ADMITTED FOR THE FIRST FEW
YEARS ONLY) OF THE FIRST CATECHISM CLASS AT ST.
MARY'S ACADEMY PROUDLY POSE WITH SISTERS OF
LORETTO AND BISHOP MACHEBEUF IN 1864.
PHOTO: DENVER PUBLIC LIBRARY,
WESTERN HISTORY DEPARTMENT

COLORADO STATE CAPITOL

200 EAST COLFAX AVENUE

Architectural style: FEDERAL REVIVAL
Built: 1886–1908
Architects: ELIJAH E. MYERS AND FRANK E. EDBROOKE

Colorado's classic domed capitol was inspired by the nation's Capitol. Massive gray granite walls support the building in the shape of a Greek cross. Four stories of government offices and galleries reside under a tower and dome plated with 24-carat Colorado gold leaf. Elijah Myers originally planned a figure depicting Colorado's "most beautiful woman" to crown the dome, but the legislature failed to agree upon the best model. The interior's grand entries, hallways, and rotunda reflect the state's vast geological riches, including Beulah Red and Colorado Yule marble floors and walls.

Women's legislative history abounds inside the Capitol. Colorado boasts the first three women state legislators in the U.S.—**Frances Klock** (ca. 1844–1908), **Carrie Clyde Holly** (ca. 1859–1943), and **Clara Cressingham** (ca. 1862–1906)—each elected to the Colorado House of Representatives in 1894, the state's first election in which women could vote. The "lady legislators" joined their male colleagues in the shiny new House chambers in January 1895, insisting on new rules banning cigar smoking, hats, and foul language. By 1901, when work on the Capitol's interior was finally complete, ten women had served in the legislature, including a social activist from North Denver, **Martha Bushnell Conine** (1881–1910). In 1913 the Colorado Senate swore in its first woman, **Helen Ring Robinson** (d. 1923), who sponsored early minimum wage, food safety, and child protection laws. The "ladies' lobby," led by **Sarah Platt Decker** (1852–1912) (Tour Five, stop 3) and the Colorado Federation of Women's Clubs, occupied their own Capitol office to review proposed legislation in the early 1900s.

Sixteen stained-glass portraits form the state's Hall of Fame inside the Capitol dome. National Jewish Hospital founder **Frances Wisebart Jacobs** (1843–1892) (see stop 2) appears as the only woman in the dome. Stained-glass portraits in the Senate Chambers include former state treasurer **Virginia Neal Blue** (1910–1975) and former state senator

An imposing dome plated with 24-carat gold leaf dominates Colorado's classic four-story Federal Revival granite Capitol.

Colorado elected America's earliest female state legislators after women won the right to vote by state referendum in 1893. The first ten women to serve in the state house are pictured in 1900.

Photo: Denver Public Library, Western History Department

Ruth Small Stockton (1916–1990). A window on the second floor central balcony honors the founder of Denver's Opportunity School, **Emily Griffith** (1868–1947) (Tour Three, stop 4).

The hand-stitched *Women's Gold* tapestry in the capitol's first-floor rotunda, depicts historic Colorado women. During the state's 1976 centennial celebration, more than 3,500 women and men created this 12-by-9-foot hanging, which immortalizes philanthropist **Helen G. Bonfils** (1889–1972), symphony conductor **Dr. Antonia Brico** (1902–1989), black pioneer **Clara Brown** (1800–1885), saintly **Mother Frances Xavier Cabrini** (1850–1917) (Tour Four, stop 2), *Harvey* author **Mary Coyle Chase** (1906–1981), entrepreneur **Mary Hauck Elitch Long** (1856–1936) (Tour Four, stop 3), public health leader **Dr. Florence Rena Sabin** (1871–1953), and others.

The Closing Era, a bronze sculpture of a Native American hunter by artist Preston Powers, stands on the east lawn. The work was commissioned by women led by First Lady **Eliza Pickrell (Mrs. John L.) Routt** (1839–1907) in 1893, the year she became the first registered woman voter in Colorado.

13   # SADIE LIKENS MONUMENT
SOUTHEAST CORNER OF EAST COLFAX AVENUE
AND BROADWAY

The busy bus stop at Colfax and Broadway obscures a 6-foot-high granite monument to **Sadie Morehouse Likens** (1840–1920), erected by the Grand Army of the Republic (American war veterans) in 1923. She was a Civil War nurse, a matron in Denver's Woman's Christian Temperance Union (WCTU) homeless shelter for women, and in 1888 the city's first police matron. Likens also directed the Florence Crittenton Home (Tour Four, stop 4) and the WCTU's Colorado Cottage Home for unwed mothers. She served as a nurse during the Spanish-American War and in the Women's Relief Corps during World War I before she died in 1920.

For more information, see *Geology Tour of Denver's Buildings and Monuments*.

THE ELEGANT INTERIOR OF THE CAPITOL FEATURES MORE
THAN THIRTY-FOUR STAINED-GLASS WINDOWS,
INCLUDING FOUR HONORING COLORADO WOMEN.

IN MEMORY OF
SADIE M. LIKENS
1840 – 1920
WHO DEVOTED MANY
YEARS OF HER LIFE
AIDING THE SURVIVORS
OF THE CIVIL WAR AND
OTHER WARS.

ERECTED A.D. 1923
BY THE
GRAND ARMY
OF THE REPUBLIC
AFFILIATED ORDERS.
AND FRIENDS.

THE SADIE LIKENS
MONUMENT ON THE
CAPITOL GROUNDS
HONORS DENVER'S
WCTU LEADER
AND FIRST
POLICE MATRON.

TOUR THREE
CIVIC CENTER, DOWNTOWN, LOWER DOWNTOWN, AND AURARIA

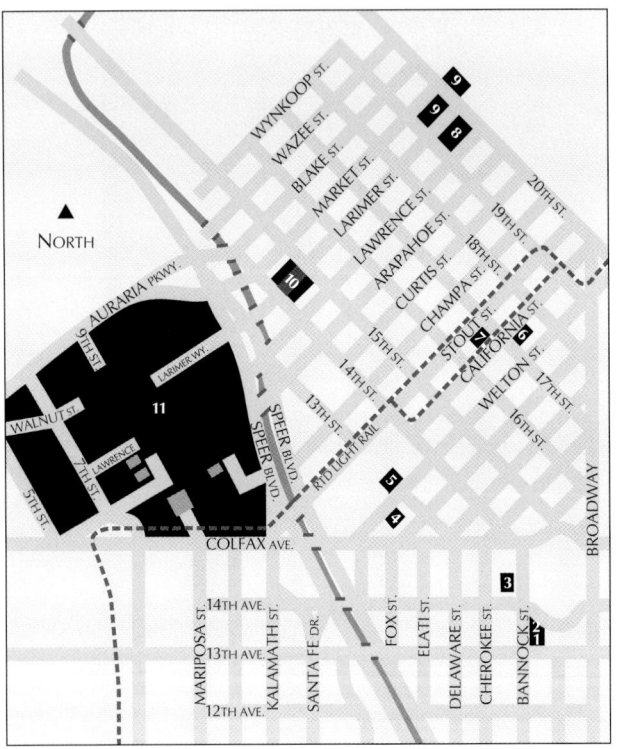

KEY

1. 1310 Bannock St. (Byers-Evans House Museum)
2. 100 West 14th Ave. (Denver Art Museum)
3. 1437 Bannock St. (Denver City and County Building)
4. 1250 Welton St. (Emily Griffith Opportunity School)
5. Welton and 13th Sts. (Women's Wall, Denver Convention Center)
6. Wells Fargo Bank Plaza, 17th and California Sts. (Colorado Woman Suffrage Association Plaque/Unity Church)
7. 730 17th St. (Equitable Building)
8. 1947 Lawrence St. (Tri-State/Denver Buddhist Temple)
9. Market St. between 19th and 21st Sts. (Denver's Historic "Red Light" District)
10. Larimer St. between 14th and 15th Sts. (Larimer Square Historic District/Crawford Building)
11. Speer Blvd. to 5th St., West Colfax Ave. to Auraria Pkwy. (Auraria Higher Education Center)

BYERS-EVANS HOUSE MUSEUM

1310 BANNOCK STREET

Architectural style: ITALIAN RENAISSANCE/ITALIANATE
Built: 1883, 1895–1902 (ADDITION), 1989 (RESTORATION)
Architects: LONG HOEFT ARCHITECTS (RESTORATION)

This informative house museum, operated by the Colorado Historical Society, depicts the lives of the city's early "movers and shakers": the Byers family and the Evans family. The home was built in 1883 for *Rocky Mountain News* founder William Newton Byers and his wife, **Elizabeth Sumner Byers** (1834–1920), who launched dozens of Denver's earliest charities. In 1889, William Gray and **Cornelia Gray Evans** (1863–1955) purchased the home. William was the son of Colorado's second territorial governor and founder of the University of Denver, John Evans, and philanthropist **Margaret Gray Evans** (1830–1906). Margaret and her daughter, Denver Art Museum founder **Anne Evans** (1871–1941), resided in the home after 1900 in a two-story brick addition. Original furnishings, including remnants of Anne's collection of southwestern Indian and Hispanic artifacts, appear throughout the home. Interactive video exhibits depict the history of Denver in the former servants' quarters.

Each of the women who resided in the home generously donated her wealth and time to serve the less fortunate and launch community arts and educational institutions. Elizabeth "Libby" Byers formed the Ladies Union Aid Society in 1860, Denver's first charitable organization. The society established the "Old Ladies' Home" for indigent women at 8th Avenue and Logan Street, a three-story brick structure that was razed in 1897. Elizabeth and Margaret Gray Evans spearheaded the Denver Orphans' Home in 1872, which still operates today as the Denver Children's Home at Colfax Avenue and Albion Street. Anne Evans served on Denver's Library Commission more than thirty years, and launched the Denver Art Museum (see stop 2). She and Denver University professor **Ida Kruse McFarlane** (1873–1940) restored the Central City Opera House in 1932.

THE TWO-STORY ITALIANATE BYERS-EVANS HOUSE MUSEUM DEPICTS THE PRIVATE
AND PUBLIC LIVES OF EARLY FEMALE PHILANTHROPISTS WHO RESIDED HERE.

ANNE EVANS PRESERVED AND
COLLECTED SOUTHWESTERN ART
WITH MISSIONARY ZEAL, AND
DEVOTED HER LIFE TO DENVER'S
PUBLIC ARTS INSTITUTIONS.

ELIZABETH BYERS ONCE DECLARED,
"WE PIONEER WOMEN RAISED
DENVER . . . FROM A LUSTY, NOISY
INFANT TO THE SEDATE, BEAUTIFUL
CITY SHE IS TODAY."

DENVER ART MUSEUM
100 WEST 14TH AVENUE

Architectural style: BRUTALIST
Built: 1971
Architects: GIO PONTI AND JAMES SUDLER ASSOCIATES, JOAL CRONENWETT

The Denver Artists' Club, a small group of mostly female artists and enthusiasts, assembled in 1893 as the forerunner of the Denver Art Museum (DAM). The club established galleries in scattered venues, then organized a museum board of directors. Denver's first art commissioner and museum founder, **Anne Evans** (1871–1941) (see stop 1), established Chappell House, a twenty-two-room Capitol Hill stone mansion at 1300 Logan Street (sadly razed in 1970), which served as DAM headquarters after 1925. Temporary galleries along Civic Center Park at 14th Avenue and Bannock Street preceded today's dramatic, high-rise, gray tile Gio Ponti edifice, which was completed in 1971— almost eighty years after the founding of the Artists' Club.

Many dynamic women contributed to the development of the Denver Art Museum. Anne Evans was a preservationist and avid collector of southwestern art. She donated her personal collection of nineteenth- and twentieth-century santos to DAM in 1936, and her Indian art pieces formed the core of the museum's extensive Native American arts collection. **Henrietta Bromwell** (1859–1946) served as secretary of the Denver Artists' Club from 1893 to 1898. Her compact paintings, sketchbooks, scrapbooks, diaries, and Artists' Club notes document the significant role of women in the city's early artistic life and its art museum. DAM founder and trustee **Marion Grace Hendrie** (1879–1968) contributed many pieces from her family's extensive art collection to the museum between 1958 and 1969. Museum codirector **Cile Miller Bach** (ca. 1910–1991) and her husband, Otto, oversaw construction of the massive new museum building and transfer of the collection there in 1971. Bach expanded community outreach programs until her retirement in 1974.

For more information, see *Denver: The Modern City*.

THE DENVER ART MUSEUM
(DAM), A TOWERING,
GRAY-TILED, MODERN MONOLITH,
HOUSES THE CITY'S ECLECTIC
COLLECTION OF ART.
PHOTO: © DENVER ART MUSEUM

THE DAM WAS THE 1893
BRAINCHILD OF THE DENVER
ARTISTS' CLUB, WHICH INCLUDED
PRINCIPAL FOUNDER AND ART
COMMISSIONER ANNE EVANS.
PHOTO: DENVER PUBLIC LIBRARY,
WESTERN HISTORY DEPARTMENT

DENVER CITY AND COUNTY BUILDING

1437 BANNOCK STREET

Architectural style: BEAUX ARTS
Built: 1932   Architects: ROLAND L. LINDER AND ROBERT K. FULLER, and THE ASSOCIATED ARCHITECTS OF DENVER

Mayor Robert Speer's premier monument to the "City Beautiful" dominates the west side of Denver's Civic Center Park. The City and County Building's granite foundation and walls support its Neoclassical Beaux Arts facade. Mayor Speer's widow, **Kate A. Speer** (1860–1956), donated the ten-bell carillon in the clock tower, which marks each hour with Westminster chimes. The building houses Denver's mayoral offices, City Council Chambers, and county and district courtrooms.

Works of art by women grace the hallways. On the third floor appears a bas-relief titled *Orpheus and the Animals* by Colorado sculptor **Gladys Caldwell Fisher** (1907–1952), who also sculpted two marble rams at the entrance of the historic marble post office (now Colorado Supreme Court chambers) at 19th and Stout Streets. Two 1991 works by **Susan Cooper** (1947–) depict Denver's architectural history at either end of the second-floor rotunda.

Women have long served in Denver's city government. Mayor Speer appointed **Anne Evans** (1871–1941) to head the city's first Art Commission. Journalist and suffrage leader **Ellis Meredith** (1865–1955) served as the first woman president of the Denver Election Commission from 1910 to 1915. Progressive coal mine owner **Josephine Aspenwall Roche** (1876–1976) served as a policewoman and social worker, working closely with Judge Ben Lindsey's innovative Juvenile Court.

Mayor Quigg Newton's reform administration appointed **Dr. Florence Rena Sabin** (1871–1953) to head the city's first Department of Health and Charities in the late 1940s. Sabin's war against tuberculosis and infant death earned her a place of honor in Statuary Hall in the nation's Capitol. Newton also recruited Native American activist **Helen Louise White Peterson** (1915–2000) to head the city's first Human Relations Commission in 1948. She exposed unhealthy slum conditions and

THE SLENDER CLOCK AND CARILLON TOWER ALLOWS DRAMATIC VIEWS OF THE ROCKY MOUNTAINS BEHIND DENVER'S ELEGANT BEAUX ARTS HOUSE OF GOVERNMENT.

COLUMBIA UNIVERSITY GRADUATE JOSEPHINE ROCHE HELPED REFORM DENVER'S PROGRESSIVE-ERA CITY GOVERNMENT AROUND 1910.

PHOTO: REPRESENTATIVE WOMEN OF COLORADO

oversaw the city's first public housing developments. Mayor Federico Peña placed preservation architect **Jennifer Moulton** in charge of the City Planning Department in 1983. The Denver Women's Commission, directed by **Chaer Robert**, was established in 1985.

An Italian-American Republican from North Denver, **Elisa Damascio Palladino** (1885–1951), served as Denver's first city councilwoman, appointed to fill a vacancy by Mayor George Begole in 1935. Four decades later, in 1975, Democrats **Cathy Donohue** and **Cathy Reynolds** became the first women elected to City Council. East High graduate **Allegra "Happy" Haynes** (1953–), who has served as City Council president, was elected the city's first African-American councilwoman in 1990. **Deborah Ortega** and **Ramona M. Martinez** have represented Denver's largest Mexican-American neighborhoods since 1987.

Stephanie Foote was appointed deputy mayor and manager of Public Works by Mayor Wellington Webb in 2000, the highest-ranking woman ever to serve in Denver city government.

For more information, see *Geology Tour of Denver's Buildings and Monuments*.

(LEFT) JOURNALIST ELLIS MEREDITH ORGANIZED COLORADO'S VICTORIOUS 1893 SUFFRAGE CAMPAIGN, THEN BECAME DENVER'S FIRST WOMAN ELECTION COMMISSIONER. (BELOW LEFT) DR. FLORENCE SABIN HEADED DENVER'S FIRST DEPARTMENT OF HEALTH.

PHOTOS: REPRESENTATIVE WOMEN OF COLORADO; DENVER PUBLIC LIBRARY, WESTERN HISTORY DEPARTMENT

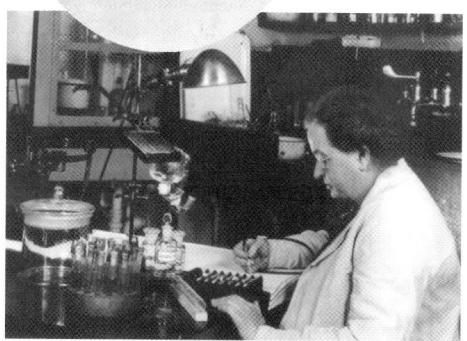

(ABOVE) COUNCILWOMAN DEBORAH ORTEGA HAS SERVED SINCE 1987. (RIGHT) ALLEGRA "HAPPY" HAYNES WAS ELECTED DENVER'S FIRST AFRICAN-AMERICAN COUNCILWOMAN IN 1990.

PHOTOS: COURTESY OF DEBORAH ORTEGA, ALLEGRA "HAPPY" HAYNES

EMILY GRIFFITH OPPORTUNITY SCHOOL

1250 WELTON STREET

Architectural style: INSTITUTIONAL

Built: 1882, 1925, 1933 Architect: UNKNOWN

"Public Opportunity School for Those Who Wish to Learn" read the sign at the entrance of "Miss Emily" Griffith's new vocational school, established in 1916 in the refurbished 1882 Longfellow grade school on Welton Street. Denver Public Schools and the state of Colorado still operate the school in a patchwork of replacement buildings at the same site. More than one million full- and part-time adult students of all ages, races, colors, and creeds have taken courses in welding, power sewing, typing, video production, and other vocational skills. Many others have pursued English-language or high school–equivalency diplomas.

Emily Griffith (1868–1947) taught in a "soddy" schoolhouse in Broken Bow, Nebraska, then relocated to the Denver Public Schools in 1895. Her first assignment at 24th Street School in the Five Points neighborhood exposed Griffith to thousands of poor, non-English-speaking immigrant and working-class families in desperate need of educational resources. With the help of fiery, red-haired *Denver Post* columnist **Frances "Pinkie" Wayne** (1870–1951), Griffith persuaded a reluctant Denver School Board to implement her experiment in free, practical vocational education for adults. Griffith received an initial salary of $1,800 per year as principal, and a budget to hire five teachers.

Griffith remained the Opportunity School's beloved principal until her sudden retirement in 1933. She and her sister Florence lived paupers' lives in a small mountain cabin at Pinecliffe, Colorado, surviving on a pension of $50 per month. In 1947, neighbors found the dead bodies of both women, each shot in the head. Neither law enforcement officials nor historians have ever explained the circumstances of the shocking deaths. More than 100,000 admirers attended Emily Griffith's funeral at Central Presbyterian Church.

The Emily Griffith Opportunity School, a four-story red brick institution, has provided job and life skills to Denverites since its founding in 1916.

Emily Griffith, a devoted educator, is memorialized in stained glass in Colorado's State Capitol.

5   WOMEN'S WALL, DENVER CONVENTION CENTER
WELTON AND 13TH STREETS
Artist: BARBARA JO REVELLE   Completed: 1991

More than eighty faces of Colorado's hidden heroines peer out from the Denver Convention Center's east exterior wall. The City of Denver commissioned University of Colorado art professor **Barbara Jo Revelle** (1946–) to design A *People's History of Colorado*, two massive tile mosaics—one for the state's legendary historic men, the other for its women. Revelle adapted images from historic photographs, then converted pixels to tiles of white, black, and shades of gray. The mural depicts women from a wide array of ethnic, racial, educational, economic, and religious backgrounds. Revelle worked for over three years to complete the murals, which span over one city block.

6   COLORADO WOMAN SUFFRAGE ASSOCIATION PLAQUE/UNITY CHURCH
WELLS FARGO BANK PLAZA,
17TH AND CALIFORNIA STREETS

Denver's Unity Church, founded in 1873 at its first site at 17th and California Streets, served Unitarian parishioners until they constructed a new building at 19th Avenue and Broadway in 1887. Neither building still stands. Unity Church was the parish of **Augusta Pierce Tabor** (1833–1895), boardinghouse proprietor and first wife of mining's "Silver King," Horace W. Tabor.

The Colorado Woman Suffrage Association met at Unity Church to plan and execute the state's first suffrage referendum in 1877. Although the measure went down in resounding defeat, Colorado women rebounded, and won full voting rights through a second referendum in 1893. Colorado congresswoman **Patricia Scott Schroeder** (1940–) dedicated a plaque to these heroic suffragists at the historic Unity Church site, now Wells Fargo Bank Plaza, during the state's centennial in 1976.

ARTIST BARBARA JO REVELLE
HAS MEMORIALIZED DOZENS
OF COLORADO'S HISTORIC
WOMEN FROM ALL WALKS
OF LIFE IN THIS
BLOCK-LONG TILE MOSAIC.

THE ORIGINAL UNITY CHURCH,
WHERE AUGUSTA TABOR
WORSHIPED, STOOD ON
CALIFORNIA STREET FROM
1873 TO 1887.
PHOTO: DENVER PUBLIC LIBRARY,
WESTERN HISTORY DEPARTMENT

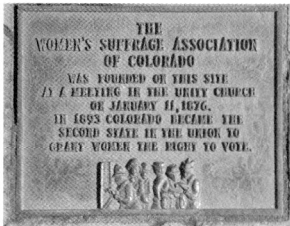

THE
WOMEN'S SUFFRAGE ASSOCIATION
OF COLORADO
WAS FOUNDED ON THIS SITE
AT A MEETING IN THE UNITY CHURCH
ON JANUARY 11, 1876.
IN 1893 COLORADO BECAME THE
SECOND STATE IN THE UNION TO
GRANT WOMEN THE RIGHT TO VOTE.

HIDDEN AMONG THE SURFACE BRICKS
AT THE EDGE OF WELLS FARGO PLAZA,
A SMALL BRONZE PLAQUE HONORS
THE 1876 COLORADO WOMEN'S [SIC]
SUFFRAGE ASSOCIATION'S EFFORTS
TO WIN THE RIGHT TO VOTE.

EQUITABLE BUILDING

730 17TH STREET

Architectural style: ITALIAN RENAISSANCE REVIVAL
Built: 1892 Architects: ANDREWS, JACQUES AND RANTOUL

This elegant nine-story office building in Denver's 17th Street financial district was once the centerpiece of "the Wall Street of the Rockies." A two-story granite foundation with rows of arched windows supports the upper stories of gray brick, designed in an E-formation. Marble from Colorado, Italy, and France covers the floors, walls, and ceilings of the building's lobbies. The Women's Bank of Colorado rekindled interest in the building when it opened Denver's first woman-owned bank there in 1976.

One of the Equitable Building's most noteworthy tenants was pioneer woman attorney **Mary Florence Lathrop** (1865–1951). In 1896, Lathrop was the second woman to receive a law degree from the University of Denver Law School. She was affectionately called "That Damned Woman" by her male colleagues. When Lathrop rented a three-room suite in the basement of the Equitable Building for $12 per month in 1897, she recalled, "I decided to live on the bottom rung of the ladder so that if I fell off I wouldn't get hurt."

Lathrop won her first lawsuit in part because opposing counsel refused to argue against a woman. She later won a long courtroom battle and appeals over the estate of George W. Clayton, who willed over $2 million to found the Clayton College for Orphan Boys. In 1913, she was the first woman admitted to the Colorado Bar Association, and gained membership in the American Bar Association in 1917. Lathrop provided pro bono legal services to the Florence Crittenton Home for unwed mothers (Tour Four, stop 4), and served as an advisor to Juvenile Court judge Benjamin Lindsey. During World War II she provided free dinners to more than 14,000 servicemen she called "my boys."

The Colorado Women's Bar Association presents the prestigious annual Mary Lathrop Award for outstanding achievement by a female attorney.

ARCHED WINDOWS AND
ENTRANCE CONSTRUCTED
OF BRICK AND PIKES PEAK
GRANITE ARE HALLMARKS
OF THE ELEGANT
EQUITABLE
BUILDING.

PIONEER WOMAN LAWYER
MARY LATHROP, CA. 1947,
PRACTICED FROM THIS DESK AT
HER EQUITABLE BUILDING OFFICE
FOR OVER FIFTY YEARS.
PHOTO: DENVER PUBLIC LIBRARY,
WESTERN HISTORY DEPARTMENT

TRI-STATE/DENVER BUDDHIST TEMPLE
1947 LAWRENCE STREET

Architectural style: MODERN WITH ASIAN ELEMENTS
Built: 1949   Architect: TEMPLE HOYNE BUELL

The Reverend Tsshyo Ono opened the Denver Buddhist Mission in the city's decaying "red light" district at 1950 Lawrence Street in 1916. Three years later Ono purchased Jenny Rogers's former "House of Mirrors" brothel at 1942 Market Street from Denver's notorious madam, **Mattie Silks** (see stop 9). The Buddhist missionaries provided religious and social services to Japanese immigrants. In 1949 the Denver Buddhist Temple was erected at 1947 Lawrence Street, where it anchored the city's Japanese-American community after the harsh backlash against them during World War II. Today's expanded Tri-State/Denver Buddhist Temple is the centerpiece of Sakura Square, an urban renewal project developed in the 1970s to preserve the city's Japanese-American heritage.

Japanese-American women have always played a significant role in Denver's Buddhist community. The Ladies' Auxiliary, historically known as the Denver Bukkyo Fujinkai, or Buddhist Women's Association, formed in 1916 with the early mission's founding. This organization has supervised the preparation of food for temple functions, such as Sakura Matsuri, the Cherry Blossom Festival. The group has diligently preserved Japanese traditions such as ikebana, the tea ceremony, and obon (folk dances), and has taught the Japanese language. The Bukkyo Fujinkai also raises funds for maintenance and expansion of the temple's property.

(TOP) PATRIOTIC JAPANESE IMMIGRANTS, INCLUDING MRS. REVEREND ONO
(FIFTH FROM LEFT, FRONT ROW), WIFE OF THE BUDDHIST MISSION FOUNDER,
POSE AT 19TH AND LAWRENCE STREETS DURING WORLD WAR I.

PHOTO: DENVER PUBLIC LIBRARY, WESTERN HISTORY DEPARTMENT

(BOTTOM) GATES OPEN INTO A PEACEFUL JAPANESE GARDEN AT THE
TRI-STATE/DENVER BUDDHIST TEMPLE, LOCATED IN SAKURA SQUARE.

DENVER'S HISTORIC "RED LIGHT" DISTRICT
MARKET STREET BETWEEN 19TH AND 21ST STREETS

MATTIE SILKS HOUSE (2009 MARKET STREET)   **D⬛L**
Architectural style: ITALIANATE
Built: 1886 Architect: UNKNOWN

JENNY ROGERS' HOUSE OF MIRRORS/MATTIE'S RESTAURANT
(1942 MARKET STREET)
Architectural style: QUEEN ANNE
Built: 1888 Architect: WILLIAM QUAYLE

Prostitution flourished in Denver from the city's founding in 1858 until 1912, when social reformers restricted this lucrative if exploitative industry. After 1889, the name "Market Street" became synonymous with the city's demimonde.

Historians estimate that more than 1,000 women worked on Market Street during its heyday. Patrons chose from a dazzling array of brothels, saloons, beer halls, peep shows, and vaudeville entertainment. Industrialized steam laundries, where women worked twelve-hour days in 95-degree temperatures for $5 per week, were conveniently located nearby.

Two important woman-owned historic brothels have been restored on today's Market Street in the heart of Denver's Lower Downtown District. Mattie Silks, Denver's famous "Queen of the Row," owned many establishments. Silks, whose real name was **Martha A. Ready** (1848–1929), employed hundreds of women. Her former brothel at 2009 Market Street has been handsomely restored to offices at the Mattie Silks Building.

Jenny Rogers, a.k.a. **Leah J. Wood** (d. 1909), Mattie Silks's toughest competitor, built her House of Mirrors in 1888 at 1942 Market Street. This opulent parlor house with wall-sized mirrors and sparkling chandeliers boasted Denver's finest poolroom. The Reverend T. Ono, head of the Denver Buddhist Mission (see stop 8), recycled the House of Mirrors in 1919 as a center for Japanese-American immigrants.

MATTIE SILKS WAS KNOWN AS DENVER'S "QUEEN OF THE ROW."
PHOTO: COLORADO HISTORICAL SOCIETY

(ABOVE LEFT) HUNDREDS OF WOMEN WORKED AT MATTIE SILKS'S BROTHEL IN THE 1890s AND EARLY 1900s. THE BUILDING NOW HOUSES UPSCALE OFFICE SPACE NEAR COORS FIELD.

(LEFT) MATTIE'S RESTAURANT, A POPULAR LoDo HAUNT, WAS ONCE JENNY ROGERS' HOUSE OF MIRRORS, MARKET STREET'S MOST ELEGANT BROTHEL.

LARIMER SQUARE HISTORIC DISTRICT/CRAWFORD BUILDING

NOR DOL

LARIMER STREET BETWEEN 14TH AND 15TH STREETS

Architectural style: VARIOUS

Built: 1870–1880s, 1965 (RESTORATION), 1990 (RESTORATION)

Architects: LANGDON MORRIS (1965 RESTORATION), SEMPLE BROWN MORRIS (1990 RESTORATION)

Denver's grande dame of historic preservation and Historic Denver, Inc. founder **Dana Hudkins Crawford** (1931–) pooled her vision, political savvy, and financial resources to preserve this charming pocket of antique buildings. The Victorian-style block was born during Denver's nineteenth-century mining boom and located within the city's founding town site on the banks of Cherry Creek. The antique storefronts now house trendy clothing shops, gourmet restaurants, and coveted office space. Crawford's successful Larimer Square project has inspired the miraculous "slums to riches" revitalization of Denver's entire Lower Downtown district. A storefront at 1439–1441 Larimer Street was renamed the Crawford Building in her honor.

Born in Salina, Kansas, Crawford graduated from Monticello College, then attended business school at the University of Kansas and Harvard/Radcliffe College. She married John Crawford in Denver in 1954, and raised four sons in the Capitol Hill neighborhood. Hoping to slow the rapid loss of Denver's architectural legacy due to urban renewal projects, the Crawfords and architect Langdon Morris took on Larimer Square as a model preservation project in 1965.

Crawford broke new ground as a savvy woman real estate developer and formed her own company, called Urban Neighborhoods, to restore and develop other landmarks. Her restoration projects have included the Oxford Hotel at 1600 16th Street in 1980, the Ice House near Union Station in 1986, and an abandoned early twentieth-century flour mill along the South Platte River in 1998, the Flour Mill Lofts on Little Raven Street. Colorado Preservation, Inc., presents the Dana Crawford Award for Outstanding Achievement in Historic Preservation in Colorado each year.

PRESERVATIONIST DANA CRAWFORD RESCUED
LARIMER SQUARE FROM URBAN RENEWAL
IN 1965, INCLUDING THIS 1875
SECOND EMPIRE CRAWFORD
BUILDING STOREFRONT (ABOVE).
PHOTO BY JIM MILMOE (RIGHT)

AURARIA HIGHER EDUCATION CENTER
SPEER BOULEVARD TO 5TH STREET, WEST COLFAX
AVENUE TO AURARIA PARKWAY

Built: 1976 Architect: JACQUES BROWNSON

NINTH STREET PARK HISTORIC DISTRICT   N☒R D☒L
Architectural style: VARIETY, INCLUDING SECOND EMPIRE, ITALIANATE,
CARPENTER GOTHIC, AND BRICK BUNGALOW
Built: 1850–1924 Architect: EDWARD D. WHITE, JR. (1976 RESTORATION)

GOLDA MEIR HOUSE   D☒L
1146 9TH STREET
Architectural style: DUPLEX
Built: 1911 Architect: UNKNOWN

ST. CAJETAN'S CENTER   D☒L
900 LAWRENCE STREET
Architectural style: SPANISH MISSION REVIVAL
Built: 1926 Architect: ROBERT WILLISON

ST. ELIZABETH'S CHURCH   N☒R D☒L
1062 11TH STREET
Architectural style: ROMANESQUE REVIVAL/GOTHIC
Built: 1898 Architect: FREDERICK W. PAROTH

Urban renewal removed over 150 acres of some of Denver's oldest working-class residential streets in the 1970s, to build the state's largest higher education center. The Auraria campus accommodates more than 34,000 mobile scholars per day, and encompasses three institutions: Community College of Denver, Metropolitan State College of Denver, and University of Colorado at Denver.

Two rows of charming brick and wood-framed residences built between 1870 and 1905 along historic Ninth Street Park preserve a remnant of the neighborhood's rich history. The vernacular clapboard–style Smedley House, built at 1020 9th Street around 1872, became one of Denver's most popular Mexican-American eateries, the Casa Mayan

(TOP) MAGDELENA GALLEGOS AND HER FAMILY POSE IN FRONT
OF GARDNER HOUSE ON 9TH STREET IN THE 1950s.
PHOTO: COURTESY OF MAGDELENA GALLEGOS, TOM NOEL COLLECTION

(BOTTOM) FORMER ISRAELI PRIME MINISTER GOLDA MEIR, WHO
LIVED IN THIS HUMBLE BRICK DUPLEX AS A TEENAGER, RECALLED
THAT "IT WAS IN DENVER THAT MY REAL EDUCATION BEGAN."

Restaurant, run by Ramon and **Caroline Gonzales**. The Gardner House, another 1870s wood-framed cottage at 1033 9th Street, now houses the Institute for Women's Studies and Services of Metropolitan State College of Denver, which promotes women's academic programs and organizes the state's largest Women's History Month commemoration each March.

The former home of **Golda Mobovitch Meir** (1898–1978), Israel's first female prime minister, may be found at 1146 9th Street. This humble one-story brick duplex, where Meir lived as a teenager, was moved to Ninth Street Park from 1606–1608 Julian Street, in west Denver's historically Jewish neighborhood.

The former St. Cajetan's Catholic Church, a pink-and-gray stucco Spanish Mission Revival structure, dominates the center campus. Built in 1926 at the behest of a group of feisty churchwomen, this parish was the first to serve Spanish-speaking families in Denver. Historian and former resident **Magdelena Gallegos** recalls that "the lives of the Spanish-speaking people in Auraria revolved around their church." The Sisters of St. Benedict's ran the parish school and convent, as well as the Ave Maria Clinic. Parishioners saved the church from demolition during construction of the Auraria campus, where it now serves as a student event center. A newer St. Cajetan's Church has held masses at 299 South Raleigh Street in southwest Denver since 1975.

Bishop Joseph Projectus Machebeuf established St. Elizabeth's Church in 1878 for Germans, then the largest immigrant group in Denver. Irish immigrants also worshiped there, until they built St. Leo's Church nearby in 1889. Church leaders replaced the small original church with the elegant, still-standing Romanesque Revival landmark in 1898, which they constructed with rusticated rhyolite stone quarried in Castle Rock, Colorado. The Franciscan Order of nuns opened the parish school in 1888, as well as the St. Rose Residence for Women (both now replaced by the modern St. Francis Interfaith Center). These resourceful nuns panhandled in Larimer Street's saloons when funds ran low. In 1936 a more prosperous parishioner, **May Bonfils Stanton** (1883–1962), donated an inspiring Gothic monastery and courtyard for the Franciscan priests, designed by architect J. J. B. Benedict.

THE FRANCISCAN ORDER OF
NUNS RAN A SCHOOL
AND WOMEN'S RESIDENCE
FROM ST. ELIZABETH'S
CATHOLIC CHURCH,
AN ELEGANT ROMANESQUE
REVIVAL LANDMARK BUILT
OF RHYOLITE STONE FROM
CASTLE ROCK.
PHOTO BY TOM NOEL

REMINISCENT OF
HISPANIC CHURCHES IN
NEW MEXICO AND
SOUTHERN COLORADO,
ST. CAJETAN'S
CATHOLIC CHURCH
ONCE ANCHORED
DENVER'S MEXICAN-
AMERICAN COMMUNITY.

TOUR FOUR
NORTHWEST DENVER

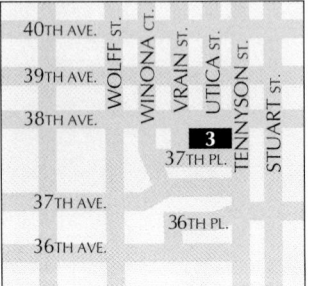

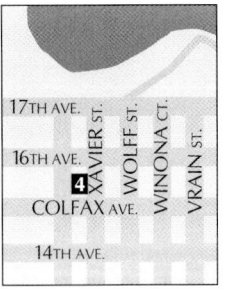

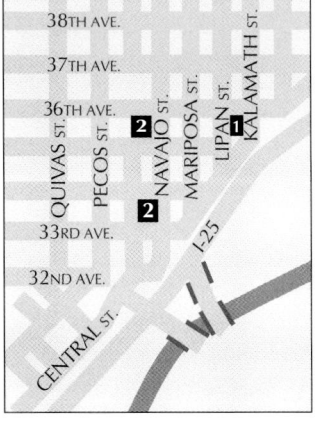

▲
North

KEY

1. 3559 Kalamath St. (Our Lady of Guadalupe Catholic Church)
2. 3549 Navajo St. (Our Lady of Mount Carmel Catholic Church)
    3357 Navajo St. (Notary House)
3. 4620 West 38th Ave. (Elitch Gardens and Theater)
4. 4901 West Colfax Ave. (Florence Crittenton Home)

OUR LADY OF GUADALUPE CATHOLIC CHURCH

DⅢL

3559 KALAMATH STREET

Architectural style: SPANISH MISSION REVIVAL

Built: 1936, 1948

Architect: JOHN K. MONROE

Our Lady of Guadalupe Catholic Church has served as a religious, social, cultural, and political center for Denver's north-side Mexican-American community since the church's founding in 1936. The Theatine Fathers established Guadalupe Church as a mission tied to St. Cajetan's parish in Auraria (Tour Three, stop 11). To honor their parishioners' Mexican heritage, the Spanish-speaking priests named the storefront mission after the most beloved female patron saint of Mexico, La Nuestra Señora de Guadalupe, and later placed her statue at the church's front entrance. The Catholic diocese built the present blond-brick Mission Revival church in 1948.

Denver-born Chicana artist **Carlota Espinoza** (1943–), whose works appear in public places throughout the city, painted an inspired mural behind the altar honoring the church's namesake in 1975. Espinoza also completed a mural entitled *Pasado, Presente, Futuro* in 1977, a brilliant depiction of the myth and reality of Chicano history and culture. This work appears at Byers branch library on Santa Fe Drive in Denver's predominantly Mexican-American west-side neighborhood.

According to religious legend, La Nuestra Señora de Guadalupe appeared to an Aztec Indian named Juan Diego near Mexico City in 1531 soon after the Spanish Conquest, and promised to protect his people. Pope John Paul II canonized Juan Diego in 2002 as the first Native American saint. The saintly red, yellow, and green image of Our Lady of Guadalupe has evolved into a popular icon representing Mexican independence from Spain, and the political and cultural identity of Mexicans and Mexican Americans. Women in Mexico and the U.S. have also adopted the symbol of Our Lady of Guadalupe to represent women's spirituality and self-determination.

THE STATUE OF THE VIRGIN OF GUADALUPE
WATCHES OVER A FIESTA IN HER HONOR AT THIS
POPULAR SPANISH MISSION–STYLE CHURCH.
PHOTO BY THOMAS H. SIMMONS,
TOM NOEL COLLECTION

INSIDE THE SANCTUARY, MURALIST CARLOTA
ESPINOZA HAS DEPICTED THE 1531 ENCOUNTER
BETWEEN NUESTRA SEÑORA DE GUADALUPE AND
A YOUNG INDIAN NEAR MEXICO CITY.

OUR LADY OF MOUNT CARMEL CATHOLIC CHURCH

NⓘR DⓘL

3549 NAVAJO STREET
Architectural style: ROMANESQUE REVIVAL
Built: 1894, 1903 Architect: FREDERICK W. PAROTH

NOTARY HOUSE (3357 NAVAJO STREET) **DⓘL**
Architectural style: LATE VICTORIAN
Built: CA. 1900 Architect: UNKNOWN

Italian immigrants, the backbone of Denver's early twentieth-century labor force, often settled in the northwest area of town known as "Little Italy." Dangers on the job, low pay, and anti-Italian prejudice impoverished the many immigrant workers and their families. Denverites of Italian descent credit a saintly woman for making their lives tolerable: **Mother Frances Xavier Cabrini** (1850–1917).

Mother Cabrini and her **Missionary Sisters of the Sacred Heart** arrived in Denver in 1902. Bishop Nicholas Matz recruited an Italian-born priest named Mariano Felice Lepore and Cabrini, who collected donations from thousands of Italian-American parishioners. They built the impressive red-brick Romanesque Our Lady of Mount Carmel Catholic Church on Navajo Street, to replace the original wood-frame church that had burned to the ground.

Mother Cabrini's first convent and school for orphan girls operated from the nearby Notary House, a small red-brick home donated in 1902 by Catholic merchant Michael Notary. The nuns took in eighteen young girls ages two to eighteen in the first year. Overcrowding prompted Cabrini to build a larger facility in 1905, Queen of Heaven Orphanage for girls, at 4825 Federal Boulevard. In 1920, the sisters opened an imposing, five-story tan-brick replacement building with a grandiose white marble statue in front. Queen of Heaven, a neighborhood landmark, survived until 1969, when it was razed to make way for Interstate 70.

The Mother Cabrini Shrine, a 22-foot statue of Jesus in the western foothills of Denver, honors the city's beloved Italian-born missionary who in 1946 became the first U.S. citizen to be canonized a saint.

"MARIA DEL CARMELINA," A 1,000-POUND BELL, ANNOUNCES EVERY MASS FROM ONE OF MOUNT CARMEL CHURCH'S MONUMENTAL COPPER-DOMED TOWERS.

MOTHER FRANCES XAVIER CABRINI AND HER SISTERS OF THE SACRED HEART FOUNDED MOUNT CARMEL CHURCH, SCHOOLS, ORPHANAGES, AND COUNTLESS INSTITUTIONS SERVING THE POOR.

PHOTO: DENVER PUBLIC LIBRARY, WESTERN HISTORY DEPARTMENT

3   # ELITCH GARDENS AND THEATER   N⬛R D⬛L
4620 WEST 38TH AVENUE

Architectural style: WESTERN STICK
Built: 1890   Architects: CHARLES HERBERT LEE AND RUDOLPH LINDEN

Mary Hauck Elitch Long (1856–1936) and her first husband, John Elitch, purchased the Chilicott Farm at West 38th Avenue and Tennyson Street in the 1880s, to supply their restaurant with fresh produce from its orchards and fields. Mary and John's gardens soon resembled a park, which inspired the couple to launch a family "resort" as a business venture. The new park opened with great fanfare on May Day 1890, complete with Denver's first zoo, vaudeville acts, and gorgeous flower gardens.

Mary took the reins of the venture when John died of pneumonia. Each year Elitch added more amusement rides to the original merry-go-round and Ferris wheel. Lush botanical and zoological gardens delighted visitors of all ages who strolled the penny arcades, picnic grounds, and walking paths. The Mulvihill-Gurtler family purchased the park during World War I after the death of Mary's second husband, Thomas D. Long. Elitch lived in a cottage on the grounds for most of her remaining years until her death in 1936.

The centerpiece of the park was the Elitch Theater, which attracted the country's top summer-stock actors and actresses, as well as vaudeville troupes and silent films. Mary Elitch counted Sarah Bernhardt, Mary Pickford, and Denver native Douglas Fairbanks, Jr., among her many friends in the theater world. For many years, Elitch turned the theater's management over to **Helen G. Bonfils** (1889–1972), D*enver Post* owner and the city's leading arts patron.

The compact, octagonal, two-story, painted wood-frame theater closed in 1987, when the Gurtlers sold the entire complex. The park's almost treeless replacement, Six Flags Elitch's Park, opened in downtown Denver's Platte River Valley in 1995. New housing developments have replaced Elitch's shade trees, flower gardens, and amusement rides, but residents have saved the Theater and Carousel Pavilion for restoration as community landmarks.

MARY ELITCH LONG FOUNDED, OWNED, AND OPERATED ELITCH GARDENS FOR OVER THIRTY YEARS.

PHOTO: REPRESENTATIVE WOMEN OF COLORADO

ELITCH THEATER, A CHARMING OCTAGONAL, WOOD-FRAME PLAYHOUSE BUILT IN 1890, OFFERED POPULAR SUMMER-STOCK PLAYS UNTIL IT CLOSED IN 1987.

FLORENCE CRITTENTON HOME
4901 WEST COLFAX AVENUE

Architectural style: INSTITUTIONAL
Built: 1899, 1913 (ADDITION), 1920 (ADDITION)
Architect: UNKNOWN

In 1892, the Woman's Christian Temperance Union (WCTU) launched an ambitious "purity campaign" at its national convention held in Denver, inspired by the "do-everything" philosophy of its dynamic leader, **Frances Elizabeth Willard** (1839–1898). In response, philanthropist Charles N. Crittenton pledged $5,000 to the Denver WCTU, in memory of his mother Florence, to establish a home for "wayward girls."

Denver's first police matron, **Sadie Morehouse Likens** (1840–1920) (Tour Two, stop 13), organized a committee who vowed to establish a "door of escape for fallen women who desire to return to a better life." In May 1893, the Florence Crittenton Home admitted its first two young women at rented facilities at 3138 Lawrence Street.

Many early residents were prostitutes seeking quick escape from abusive pimps. When policemen and physicians began referring hundreds of unwed pregnant women, the WCTU built a permanent residence on West Colfax Avenue. In 1899, Judge Benjamin Lindsey, founder of Denver's Juvenile Court, concluded that "there never was a better work established anywhere." Additions were built in 1913, and again in 1920, when lawyer **Gail Laughlin** (1868–1952) and a group of women physicians raised funds for medical facilities with operating and delivery rooms.

During the Crittenton Home's earlier decades, unwed mothers were unfairly stigmatized, and officials pressured most residents to give up their babies for adoption. Today, Human Services, Inc., and Denver Public Schools operate Florence Crittenton School in relocated facilities, as an alternative high school where teenage mothers gain independence by attending academic, parenting, and career classes during and after their pregnancy.

The Volunteers of America took over and remodeled the historic building complex in the 1980s.

POLICE MATRON SADIE LIKENS
LAUNCHED THE FLORENCE
CRITTENTON HOME IN 1893.
PHOTO: REPRESENTATIVE WOMEN
OF COLORADO

THE WOMAN'S CHRISTIAN TEMPERANCE
UNION (WCTU) FOUNDED THIS EARLY
DENVER ORPHANAGE, BATTERED
WOMEN'S SHELTERS, AND THE
FLORENCE CRITTENTON HOME,
WHICH STILL OPERATES AS A SCHOOL
FOR UNWED TEENAGE MOTHERS.
PHOTO: DENVER PUBLIC LIBRARY,
WESTERN HISTORY DEPARTMENT

TOUR FIVE
SOUTH DENVER

▲
North

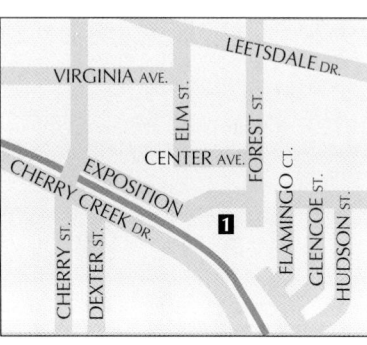

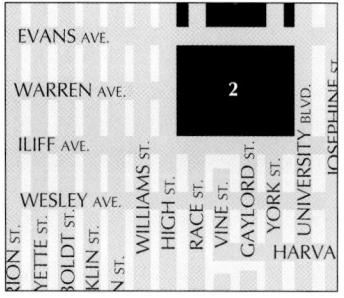

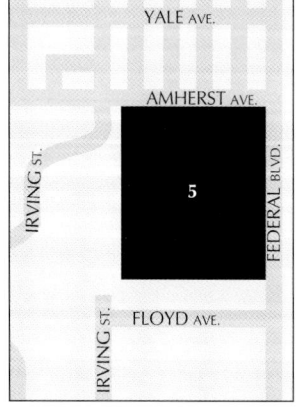

KEY

1. 715 South Forest St. (Four Mile Historic Park)
2. 2199 South University Blvd. (University of Denver Campus)
3. 1501 South Logan St. (Sarah Platt Decker Library)
4. 1510 South Grant St. (Fleming Mansion)
5. 3001 South Federal Blvd. (Teikyo Loretto Heights University, Old Main Hall)

FOUR MILE HISTORIC PARK
715 SOUTH FOREST STREET

FOUR MILE HOUSE   N■R D■L

Architectural style: LOG CABIN, FRAME, BRICK VICTORIAN
Built: 1859, 1870s, 1883, 1976 Architects: SAMUEL AND JONAS
BRANTNER (ORIGINAL), EDWARD D. WHITE, JR. (RESTORATION)

Denver's Four Mile House, a hewn-log stagecoach stop built by
gold-seekers Samuel and **Elizabeth Brantner** (1843–1882) in 1859, is
the city's oldest surviving structure. The original house, several out-
buildings, and 12 acres of orchard, park, and fields along the banks of
Cherry Creek enjoyed a major restoration in 1976 and now comprise
Four Mile Historic Park. The City and County of Denver operates this
living history museum complex.

A feisty widow, **Mary Cawker** (1813–1919), purchased Four Mile
House in 1860 and operated a popular stagecoach station, tavern, and
rustic hotel. The Cherry Creek flood of 1864 ruined Cawker's business.
She sold the flooded property for $800 to Levi and Millie Booth, who
built a successful agricultural venture.

Levi and **Millie Downing Booth** (1837–1926) arrived on a horse-drawn
wagon in 1864. Until 1870, the couple operated the stagecoach stop,
where Millie prepared meals and buckets of clean water for weary
travelers. She raised three children at the farm: Gillett, Lillie Belle, and
Ella Grace, who attended the one-room schoolhouse the Booths built
on their land.

Millie operated the Maple Grove Dairy in her cellar, delivering butter
to the finest hotels. She also produced award-winning honey out of the
"Bee House," a small bunkhouse. One year, Booth tended more than
120 bee colonies and produced 4 tons of honey.

In 1874 the Booths founded the Cherry Creek Grange, a meeting hall
for farming families (still standing at 4521 Leetsdale Drive). Millie
served on the local school board in 1888, then the only office for which
women could vote and run. Both Millie and her daughter, **Grace Booth
Working** (1868–1958), campaigned for women's suffrage in 1893.

After Levi's death in 1912, Millie managed the house and farm until
her death in 1926.

WOOD-FRAME AND BRICK ADDITIONS CONCEAL THE ORIGINAL HEWN-LOG STAGE STOP BUILT IN 1859, KNOWN AS FOUR MILE HOUSE.

PORTRAITS OF MILLIE BOOTH (CENTER) AND HER CHILDREN GILLETT (LEFT) AND GRACE (RIGHT) HANG IN THE BOOTH FAMILY HOME, NOW A MUSEUM AT FOUR MILE HISTORIC PARK.

PHOTOS BY MARCIA GOLDSTEIN

UNIVERSITY OF DENVER CAMPUS
2199 SOUTH UNIVERSITY BOULEVARD

ILIFF SCHOOL OF THEOLOGY
(2201 SOUTH UNIVERSITY BOULEVARD)
Architectural style: GOTHIC REVIVAL WITH RICHARDSONIAN ELEMENTS
Built: 1892 Architects: FULLER AND WHEELER

MARY REED BUILDING (FORMER MARY REED LIBRARY)
(2199 SOUTH UNIVERSITY BOULEVARD)
Architectural style: AMERICAN COLLEGIATE GOTHIC
Built: 1932 Architect: HARRY JAMES MANNING

MARGERY REED HALL
(EAST EVANS AVENUE AND SOUTH UNIVERSITY BOULEVARD)
Architectural style: COLLEGIATE GOTHIC
Built: 1928–1929 Architect: CHARLES Z. KLAUDER

JOSEPHINE EVANS MEMORIAL CHAPEL   N⊞R D⊞L
(WEST OF MARY REED BUILDING)
Architectural style: GOTHIC REVIVAL
Built: 1878 Architect: UNKNOWN

ROBERT AND JUDI NEWMAN CENTER FOR PERFORMING ARTS
AND LAMONT SCHOOL OF MUSIC
(2344 EAST ILIFF AVENUE)
Architectural style: POSTMODERN
Built: 2002
Architects: CABELL CHILDRESS, MARK RODGERS, ANDERSON MASON DALE

Territorial Governor John Evans founded the University of Denver (DU) in 1864, building on his experience as a founder of Northwestern University near Chicago. Colorado's oldest university also boasts Denver's earliest female graduates and woman professors. Many were pioneers in their field.

Generous female benefactors donated the bricks and mortar that formed the early backbone of the university. **Elizabeth Iliff Warren** (1845–1920), a Singer sewing machine saleswoman who inherited the

CATHEDRAL-LIKE ROWS OF GOTHIC
WINDOWS POINT SKYWARD
FROM THE MASSIVE RED
SANDSTONE LANDMARK,
THE ILIFF SCHOOL OF
THEOLOGY.

THE·ILIFF·SCHOOL·OF·THEOLOGY·

MARY DEAN REED, ARGUABLY DENVER'S
MOST GENEROUS PHILANTHROPIST, DONATED
THE HANDSOME COLLEGIATE
GOTHIC–STYLE MARY REED LIBRARY (BELOW),
LONG THE CENTERPIECE OF THE CAMPUS.

PHOTO: REPRESENTATIVE WOMEN OF COLORADO (LEFT);
PHOTO BY MARCIA GOLDSTEIN (BELOW)

Iliff cattle empire, generously endowed the Iliff School of Theology as a special school within the university in 1888. The massive four-story school was built in 1892 of rough-faced red sandstone, and loosely resembles a European cathedral with eight Gothic windows above an arched stone entryway. A contemporary addition extends to the south of the original edifice.

Mary Dean (Mrs. Verner Z.) **Reed** (1875–1945) donated over $1 million to build the handsome Margery Reed Hall in memory of her daughter in 1928. She built the monumental Mary Reed Library of more than 500,000 volumes in 1932, whose tower dominates the central quadrangle of the campus. The university's Women's College, an innovative program for working women, is currently housed in the former library, now called the Mary Reed Building.

DU founders John Evans and **Margaret Gray Evans** (1830–1906) (Tour Three, stop 1) built a Morrison sandstone chapel in memory of their daughter, **Josephine Evans Elbert** (1844–1868), at 13th Avenue and Bannock Street in 1878. The chapel was relocated stone by stone to the DU campus in the 1960s and designated an official Denver Landmark in 1974.

DU's Lamont School of Music and its namesake, **Florence Lamont Hinman** (1884–1964), pioneered music education in Denver. The Canadian-born voice teacher came to Colorado in 1912 to recover from tuberculosis. With the help of DU professor **Ida Kruse McFarlane** (1873–1940), she founded the Lamont School in 1924 as an affiliate of the university. Lamont trained hundreds of musicians from studios in the Berger mansion at East 12th Avenue and Sherman Street. Mary Reed donated the elegant Brown mansion (since demolished) at 909 Grant Street to the school in 1941. Lamont's students performed with the first Central City opera company, and she remained active in music and opera circles until her death in 1964.

DU relocated the Lamont School to the former Colorado Women's College campus in Park Hill in the 1990s (Tour Two, stop 1). The school's latest home is Virginia E. Trevorrow Hall, part of the $70 million Robert and Judi Newman Center for Performing Arts (see photo on page 3). This impressive new seven-building arts complex, built of Hansen stone with copper trim and embedded with elaborate marble murals celebrating the performing arts, was completed in 2002–2003.

FLORENCE LAMONT HINMAN (ABOVE),
THE "STAR-MAKER," TRAINED HUNDREDS
OF MUSICIANS AT THE LAMONT SCHOOL
OF MUSIC, FOUNDED WITH THE HELP OF
DU ENGLISH PROFESSOR IDA KRUSE
MCFARLANE IN 1924 (RIGHT).

PHOTOS: UNIVERSITY OF DENVER LIBRARY,
SPECIAL COLLECTIONS (ABOVE); REPRESENTATIVE
WOMEN OF COLORADO (RIGHT)

3 SARAH PLATT DECKER LIBRARY   D⬚L
1501 SOUTH LOGAN STREET

Architectural style: ELIZABETHAN COTTAGE

Built: 1913, 1993   Architects: WILLIS A. MAREAN AND ALBERT J.
NORTON, DAVID OWEN TRYBA (RESTORATION)

The Decker branch library, an inviting brick English cottage, honors one of the city's most dynamic organizers of women during the Progressive Era, **Sarah Platt Decker** (1852–1912). Sarah Sophia Chase was born and raised in Holyoke, Massachusetts. She moved to Denver in 1887 with her second husband, Colonel James H. Platt, who died suddenly. Sarah turned to charity work and Colorado's successful women's suffrage campaign in 1893. One year later, the Woman's Club of Denver elected her as its founding president, as the club aggressively undertook a variety of political, civic, and social welfare projects (Tour Two, stop 8). By 1904, Sarah Platt led the legislative committee of the Colorado Federation of Women's Clubs, and later served as national president of the General Federation of Women's Clubs. In 1912 after her second marriage, Sarah Platt Decker contemplated a run for the U.S. Senate, but her aspirations were cut short by her sudden, tragic death that year at age sixty.

4 FLEMING MANSION   D⬚L
1510 SOUTH GRANT STREET

Architectural style: QUEEN ANNE

Built: 1882   Architect: EDWARD E. WHITE (RESTORATION)

Nearby in Platte Park stands the former home of South Denver town founder James A. Fleming, built in 1882. This historic mansion served as the clubhouse of the civic-minded South Side Women's Club from 1914 to the mid-1950s. In 1957, nostalgic club members rescued the Fleming Mansion from demolition, and persuaded city officials to recycle the attractive Queen Anne rusticated stone mansion as a community center for senior citizens. Distinguished by its three conical-roofed towers, the home earned Denver Landmark status in 1973.

TERRA-COTTA TRIM AND LEADED-GLASS WINDOWS
DECORATE THE DECKER LIBRARY, A
NEIGHBORHOOD LANDMARK REMINISCENT OF
ANNE HATHAWAY'S ENGLISH COTTAGE.

THE LIBRARY WAS BUILT IN
1913 IN MEMORY OF
WOMAN'S CLUB LEADER
SARAH PLATT DECKER
(ABOVE) BY THE SOUTH
SIDE WOMEN'S CLUB,
WHICH OPERATED FROM
THE NEARBY FLEMING
MANSION (BELOW).

PHOTO: REPRESENTATIVE WOMEN
OF COLORADO (ABOVE)

TEIKYO LORETTO HEIGHTS UNIVERSITY, OLD MAIN HALL

3001 SOUTH FEDERAL BOULEVARD

Architectural style: RICHARDSONIAN ROMANESQUE
Built: 1890 Architect: FRANK EDBROOKE

Old Main, a towering red Manitou sandstone edifice, was the original home of Denver's first Catholic women's college, Loretto Heights College (LHC). Eighteen handsome, German-made stained-glass windows grace the chapel, which was added to the six-story administration and classroom building in 1910–1911.

The Sisters of Loretto, the college's founders, arrived in Denver in 1864 when they established St. Mary's Academy, Colorado's oldest continuously operating girls' school (Tour Two, stop 11). **Sister Mary Pancratia Bonfils** (1852–1915) took charge of the fledgling girls' academy in 1868. After Bonfils was appointed mother superior in 1882, she selected a hilltop in the southwestern outskirts of Denver to establish a Catholic women's college.

Mother Bonfils hired Frank Edbrooke to design Old Main Hall in 1890. The school opened a year later to fifty high school students, but did not admit college students until 1918, three years after the death of Mother Bonfils. Mary Hayden was the first college graduate, in 1921. A four-story brick building named Pancratia Hall in honor of Mother Bonfils became a college dormitory in 1941.

LHC played an important role during World War I, when the Fifth National Service School trained women at the campus for home-front duties. The Red Cross conducted training courses in military drills, calisthenics, telegraph operation, and first aid for more than 200 khaki-clad, volunteer "soldierettes."

LHC alternately thrived and struggled for seven decades. In 1988 the Jesuits at Regis College purchased, then sold, the 160-acre campus for over $6 million to Teikyo University of Tokyo, Japan. Teikyo Loretto Heights University converted historic Old Main and Pancratia Hall into administrative offices and classrooms, and has preserved the nuns' graveyard in remembrance of the school's dedicated female founders.

LORETTO HEIGHTS HOSTED A WORLD WAR I RED CROSS TRAINING FACILITY FOR WOMEN. THE VICTORIAN LANDMARK OLD MAIN HALL IS IN THE BACKGROUND.

PHOTO: DENVER PUBLIC LIBRARY, WESTERN HISTORY DEPARTMENT

PIONEER WOMEN'S EDUCATOR MOTHER MARY PANCRATIA BONFILS AND THE SISTERS OF LORETTO FOUNDED ST. MARY'S ACADEMY IN 1864, THEN LORETTO HEIGHTS COLLEGE IN 1890.

PHOTO: ST. MARY'S ACADEMY

BIBLIOGRAPHY

Bakke, Diane. *Places Around the Bases: A Historic Tour of the Coors Field Neighborhood.* Englewood, CO: Westcliffe Publishers, 1995.

Beaton, Gail M. "The Widening Sphere of Women's Lives: The Literary Study and Philanthropic Work of Six Women's Clubs in Denver, 1881–1945." *Essays and Monographs in Colorado History* 13, Denver: Colorado Historical Society, 1993.

Breck, Allen duPont. *From the Rockies to the World: The History of the University of Denver, 1864–1997.* 2d ed. Denver: University of Denver, 1997.

Bundles, A'Lelia. *On Her Own Ground: The Life and Times of Madam C. J. Walker.* New York: Washington Square Press, 2001.

Carroll, Dianna. "The History and Description of the City and County Building." Denver: Denver City Council, 1992.

Cervi, Clé, and Nancy M. Peterson. *The Women Who Made the Headlines: Denver Woman's Press Club, The First Hundred Years.* Lakewood, CO: Western Guideways, Ltd., 1998.

Coel, Margaret. *The Pride of Our People: The Colorado State Capitol.* Denver: Colorado General Assembly, 1992.

Dickson, Lynda. "Lifting as We Climb: African-American Women's Clubs of Denver, 1890–1925." *Essays and Monographs in Colorado History* 13, Denver: Colorado Historical Society, 1993.

Distinguished Colorado Women Walking Tour. Denver: Fairmount Cemetery Company, 1996.

"Doctor Justina Ford House Grand Opening and Dedication Ceremony Program," September 24, 1988. Denver: Black American West Museum and Heritage Center.

Fetter, Rosemary. *A Brief History of Auraria: Celebrating 20 Years of Innovation in Higher Education.* Denver: Auraria Higher Education Center, 1997.

Fitzharris, Mary Ann, and Jeanne Abrams, Ph.D. *A Place to Heal: The History of National Jewish Medical and Research Center.* Denver: National Jewish Medical and Research Center, 1997.

Gallegos, Magdelena. *Auraria Remembered*. Denver: Community College of Denver, 1991.

Goldstein, Marcia T. "Breaking Down Barriers: The Denver YWCA and the Phyllis Wheatley Branch." *University of Colorado at Denver Historical Studies Journal* 12(1), Spring 1995.

Goldstein, Marcia T., and Rosemary Fetter. *Let the Women Vote! Colorado Suffrage Centennial, 1893–1993*. Denver: Colorado Committee for Women's History, 1993.

Goodstein, Phil. *Denver's Capitol Hill: One Hundred Years of Life in a Vibrant Urban Neighborhood*. Denver: Life Publications, 1988.

Goodstein, Phil. *South Denver Saga*. Denver: New Social Publications, 1991.

Grinstead, Leigh A. *Molly Brown's Capitol Hill Neighborhood*. Denver: Historic Denver, Inc., 1997.

Grizzard, Justina. "Bricks and Mortar: History of Shorter." Sanctuary Dedication Program, June 24, 1990 (Denver Public Library/Western History Department).

Halaas, David Fridtjof. "The House in the Heart of a City: The Byers and Evans Families of Denver." *Colorado Heritage* 4, 1989.

Harris, Neil, Marlene Chambers, and Lewis Wingfield Story. *The First Hundred Years: The Denver Art Museum*. Denver: Denver Art Museum, 1996.

Hauck, Laura M. *Images of America: Five Points Neighborhood of Denver*. Chicago: Arcadia Publishing, 2001.

Hendricks, Rickey, and Mark S. Foster. *For a Child's Sake: History of the Children's Hospital, Denver, Colorado, 1910–1990*. Niwot: University Press of Colorado, 1994.

Iverson, Kristen. *Molly Brown: Unraveling the Myth*. Boulder, CO: Johnson Books, 1999.

Jarrett, Carl. *The Stained Glass Windows of the Colorado State Senate Chamber*. Denver: Colorado State Senate, 2000.

Leonard, Stephen J., and Thomas J. Noel. *Denver: Mining Camp to Metropolis*. Niwot: University Press of Colorado, 1990.

Noel, Thomas J. *Buildings of Colorado*. New York: Oxford University Press, 1997.

Noel, Thomas J. *Colorado Catholicism and the Archdiocese of Denver, 1857–1998*. Niwot: University Press of Colorado, 1989.

Noel, Thomas J. *Denver Landmarks & Historic Districts: A Pictorial Guide*. Niwot: University Press of Colorado, 1996.

Noel, Thomas J. *Denver's Larimer Street: Main Street, Skid Row and Urban Renaissance*. Denver: Historic Denver, Inc., 1982.

Noel, Thomas J., and Barbara S. Norgren. *Denver: The City Beautiful and Its Architects*. Denver: Historic Denver, Inc., 1987.

Peters, Bette D. *Denver's Four Mile House*. Denver: Golden Bell Press, 1980.

Semple, James Alexander. *Representative Women of Colorado*. Denver: Alexander Art Publishing Co., 1914.

Smith, Jean Walton, and Elaine Colvin Walsh. *Queen of the Hill: The Private Life of the Colorado Governor's Mansion*. Denver: Volunteers of the Colorado Historical Society, 1979.

Student, Annette L. "Sadie Likens: Patron of the Fallen." *Colorado Heritage*, Summer 2001.

Symons, Clé Cervi. *100 Moore Years, 1890–1990: A History of Dora Moore School*. Denver, 1990.

Turner, Wallace B. *Colorado Women's College: The Story of a Dream*. Marceline, MO: Walsworth Publishing Company, 1982.

Van Wyke, Millie. *The Town of South Denver: Its People, Neighborhoods and Events Since 1858*. Boulder, CO: Pruett Publishing Company, 1991.

Varnell, Jeanne. *Women of Consequence: The Colorado Women's Hall of Fame*. Boulder, CO: Johnson Books, 1999.

Walker, Elizabeth Owen. *Cast in Stone: The Molly Brown House Revealed*. Denver: Historic Denver, Inc., 2001.

Wiberg, Ruth Eloise. *Rediscovering Northwest Denver: Its History, Its People, Its Landmarks*. Niwot: University Press of Colorado, 1995.

Working, Gertrude Brown. *Levi Booth of Four Mile House*. Denver: Gertrude Brown Working, 1986.

VIRGINIA NEAL BLUE (1910–1970) SERVED AS COLORADO STATE TREASURER FROM 1966 TO 1970. SHE APPEARS IN STAINED GLASS IN THE SENATE CHAMBERS OF THE STATE CAPITOL (SEE TOUR TWO, STOP 12).

INDEX

Addams, Jane, 26

African Americans, 10, 12, 16, 18, 20, 30, 58, 59, 98

Agnes Reid Tammen Hall/Children's Hospital, 32

Andrews, Jacques and Rantoul, 64

Associated Architects of Denver, The, 56

Auraria Higher Education Center (AHEC), 72–75

Autry Museum of Western Heritage, 2, 4

Ave Maria Clinic/St. Cajetan's Catholic Church, 74

Axtens, S. Arthur, 24

Baby's Summer Hospital, 32

Bach, Cile Miller, 54

Baptist Women's Auxiliary, 24

Bates, Dr. Mary Barker, 38

Beaumont Nurses' Home (National Jewish Hospital), 28

Bee House/Four Mile Historic Park, 88

Benedict, J. J. B., 74

Bernhardt, Sarah, 82

Black American West Museum and Heritage Center, 12

Blue, Virginia Neal, 46, 101

B'nai B'rith Building (National Jewish Hospital), 28–29

Boettcher, Edna Case (Mrs. Claude), 36

Bonfils, Belle Barton (Mrs. Frederick G.), 32

Bonfils, Helen G., 14, 48, 82

Bonfils, Mother Mary Pancratia, 6, 44, 96–97

Bonfils Stanton, May, 74

Booth, Millie Downing (Mrs. Levi), 88–89

Brantner, Elizabeth, 88

Brantner, Samuel and Jonas, 88

Brico, Dr. Antonia, 48

Bromwell, Henrietta, 54

Brooker, Kathleen, 7

brothels, 66, 68

Brown, "Aunt" Clara, 48

Brown, Margaret Tobin "Molly" (Mrs. J. J.), 6, 42–43, 44, 99, 100

Brownson, Jacques, 72

Buddhist Mission, Denver, 66–68

Buddhist Women's Association, Denver, 66

Buell, Temple Hoyne, 66

THIS WINDOW IN THE STATE CAPITOL
HONORS RUTH SMALL STOCKTON
(1916–1990), WHO SERVED IN BOTH
HOUSES OF THE COLORADO LEGISLATURE
FOR TWENTY-FOUR YEARS, FROM 1960
TO 1984 (SEE TOUR TWO, STOP 12).

Bukkyo Fujinkai/Buddhist Women's
   Association, 66
Byers branch library, 78
Byers, Elizabeth Sumner (Mrs. William
   N.), 52–53, 99
Byers-Evans House Museum, 52–53

Cabrini, Mother Frances Xavier, 6, 48,
   80–81
Casa Mayan Restaurant, 72, 74
Cawker, Mary, 88
Central City Opera House, 52, 92
Charity Organization Society, 28
Chase, Mary Coyle, 48
Cheesman, Alice Foster (Mrs. Walter
   Scott), 36
Cheesman-Evans-Boettcher Mansion, 36
Cherry Creek Grange, 88
Children's Hospital, 32–33
Childress, Cabell, 90
City and County Building, Denver, 56–58
City Park, 30
Civic Center Park, 54, 56
Cleo Parker Robinson Dance School
   and Theater, 20–21
Closing Era, The, sculpture, 48
Collins, Judy, 34
Colorado Cottage Home, 48

Colorado Equal Suffrage Association, 40
Colorado Federation of Women's Clubs,
   38, 46, 94
Colorado Governor's Residence, 36–37
Colorado Historical Society, 52
Colorado Preservation, Inc., 70
Colorado State Capitol, 46–49, 61, 98
Colorado Woman Suffrage Association,
   62–63
Colorado Women's Bar Association, 64
Colorado Women's College, 2, 5, 20,
   24–27, 92, 99
Community College of Denver, 72
Conine, Martha Bushnell, 46
Cooper, Susan, 56
Corona School (Dora Moore School), 34
Courlis, Judge Rebecca Love, 36
Crawford Building, 70–71
Crawford, Dana Hudkins, 7, 70–71
Cressingham, Clara, 46
Cronenwett, Joal, 54
Cushman, Oca Rush, 32

Dale, Anderson Mason, 90
Decker Library, 94–95
Decker, Sarah Platt, 38, 46, 94–95
Denison, Ella Strong, 38
Denver Art Museum, 52, 54–55
Denver Artists' Club, 54
Denver Buddhist Mission, 66–67, 68
Denver Buddhist Temple, 66–67
Denver Children's Home, 52
Denver Convention Center, 62
Denver Maternity and Women's
   Hospital, 32
Denver Orphans' Home, 52

Denver Public Schools, 20, 34, 60, 84

Denver Sheltering Home for Jewish Children, 28

Denver Woman's Press Club (DWPC), 40–41

Denver Women's Commission, 58

DePriest, Ida, 18

Diego, Juan, 78

Donohue, Cathy, 58

Dora Moore School, 34–35

Douglass, Frederick, 30

Dwight, Ed, 30–31

Edbrooke, Frank E., 46, 96

Eisenhower, Mamie Doud, 34

Elbert, Josephine Evans, 92

Elitch Carousel Pavilion, 82

Elitch Long, Mary Hauck, 48, 82–83

Elitch Theater, 82–83

Emily Griffith Opportunity School, 48, 60–61

Espinoza, Carlota, 78–79

Evans, Anne, 7, 52–56

Evans, Cornelia Gray (Mrs. William), 52

Evans Elbert, Josephine, 92

Evans, Gladys Cheesman, 36

Evans, John 52, 90

Evans, Margaret Gray (Mrs. John), 52, 92

Fentress and Associates, Curtis W., 12

Fifth National Service School, 96–97

Fisher, Gladys Caldwell, 56

Five Points neighborhood, 10, 12, 17, 18, 60

Fleming Mansion, 94–95

Florence Crittenton Home, 48, 64, 84–85

Flour Mill Lofts, 70

Foote Hall, Colorado Women's College, 24, 26–27

Foote, Margaret Sharpless, 26

Foote, Retta Ann, 26

Foote, Stephanie, 58

Ford, Dr. Justina Warren, 6, 12–13

Four Mile House and Historic Park, 88–89

Franciscan Order of nuns, 74–75

Fuller and Wheeler, 90

Fuller, Robert K., 56

Gallegos, Magdalena, 73–74

Gandhi, Mahatma, 30

Gardner House/Ninth Street Park, Auraria Campus, 73–74

General Federation of Women's Clubs 38, 94

George Washington Carver Day Nursery, 18–19

German immigrants, 74

Golda Meir House/Auraria Campus, 72, 74

Gonzales, Caroline, 74

Griffith, Emily, 6, 48, 60–61

Hayden, Mary, 96

Haynes, Allegra "Happy," 58–59

Hendrie, Marion Grace, 54

Hinman, Florence Lamont, 92–93

Historic Denver, Inc., 12, 14, 42, 70

Holly, Carrie Clyde, 46

House of Mirrors brothel, 66, 68–69

Iliff, Elizabeth (Warren), 90

Iliff School of Theology, 90–92

Indian women, 6–7

Institute for Women's Studies and Services of Metropolitan State College, 74

Ireland and Parr, 20

Irish immigrants, 74

Italian immigrants, 80

Jack, Bessie, 14

Jackson, Frank H., 24

Jacobs, Frances Wisebart, 28–29, 46

Japanese Americans, 66

Japanese immigrants, 66–68

Johnson & Wales (J&W) University, 24, 26

Johnson, Gertrude I., 26

Josephine, Evans, Memorial Chapel, 90

Juvenile Court, Denver, 38, 42, 56, 64, 84

Klauder, Charles Z., 90
Klock, Frances, 46

Ladies Union Aid Society, 52
Lamm, Dottie Venard (Mrs. Richard), 36
Lamont Hinman, Florence, 92–93
Lamont School of Music, 3, 26, 90, 92–93
Lang, William, 42
Larimer Square Historic District, 70–71
Lathrop, Esq., Mary Florence, 64–65
Laughlin Esq., Gail, 84
Lee, Charles Herbert, 82
Likens, Sadie Morehouse, 48–49, 84–85
Linden, Rudolph, 82
Linder, Roland L., 56
Lindsey, Judge Benjamin Barr, 38, 42, 56, 64, 84
Loire, Gabriel, 26
Long Hoeft Architects, 52
Long, Mary Hauck Elitch, 82–83
Lorber, Fannie Eller, 28
Loretto Heights College, 96–97
Love, Ann Daniels (Mrs. John A.), 7, 36–37, 42
Love, Dr. Minnie C. T., 32

Machebeuf, Bishop Joseph Projectus, 44–45, 74
Madam C. J. Walker Manufacturing Company, 10–11
Maes, Sister Beatrice, 44
Manning, Harry James, 14, 90
Marean, Willis A., 36, 94
Margery Reed Hall/University of Denver, 90, 92
Margery Reed Mayo Day Nursery, 14–15
Market Street "Red Light" District, 66, 68–69
Martin Luther King, Jr., Monument, 30–31
Martinez, Ramona M., 58

Mary Reed Building/University of Denver, 26, 90–92
Mattie Silks House, 68–69
Matz, Bishop Nicholas, 80
Mayo, Margery Reed, 14, 92
McFarlane, Ida Kruse, 52, 92–93
McNichols, Marjory (Mrs. Steve), 36
Meir, Golda, 73–74
Meredith, Ellis, 56, 59
Metropolitan State College of Denver, 72, 74
Mexican Americans, 58, 72–75, 78
Mile High Child Care Association, 14, 18
Molly Brown House Museum, 42–43
Monroe, John K., 78
Moore, Dora, 34
Mora, Sister Ignatia, 44
Morris, Langdon, 70
Morse, Stanley, 24
Mother Cabrini Shrine, 80
Moulton, Jennifer, 58
Mount Carmel Catholic Church, 80–81
Mountjoy and Frewan, 28
Myers, Elijah E., 46

National Association of Negro Women's Clubs, 18
National Asthma Center, 28
National Jewish Hospital, 28–29, 46
National Woman's Party, 42
Negro Women's Club Association Day Nursery, 18–19
Newman Center for Performing Arts/ University of Denver, 3, 90, 92
Newton, Quigg—Mayor of Denver, 56
Nineteenth Amendment, 40
Ninth Street Park Historic District/Auraria Campus, 72, 74
Norton, Albert J., 36, 94
Notary House, 80

Old Ladies' Home, 52
Old Main Hall/Loretto Heights College, 96–97

ADVENTUROUS DENVER WOMEN CLIMB A COTTONWOOD TREE ALONG THE SOUTH PLATTE RIVER, CA. 1890.
PHOTO: COLORADO HISTORICAL SOCIETY

Ono, Mrs. Reverend Tsshyo, 67
Ono, Reverend Tsshyo, 66, 68
Opportunity School, 60–61
Orpheus and the Animals sculpture, 56
Ortega, Debra, 58
Our Lady of Guadalupe, 14, 78–79
Our Lady of Guadalupe Catholic
    Church, 78–79
Our Lady of Mount Carmel Catholic
    Church, 80–81
Owens, Frances (Mrs. Bill), 36

Palladino, Elisa Damascio, 58
Pancratia Hall/Loretto Heights College, 96
Parks, Rosa McCauley, 30–31
Parks School of Business, 44
Paroth, Frederick W., 72, 80
Pasado, Presente, Futuro mural, 78
Peña, Federico—Mayor of Denver, 58
People's History of Colorado mural, 62–63
Peterson, Helen Louise White, 56
Phyllis Wheatley YWCA, 16–17
Pickford, Mary, 82
Pisko, Seraphine Eppstein, 28
Ponti, Gio, 54
Pope John Paul II, 78
Pouw, Stanley Associates, 34
Powers, Preston, 48

Quayle, William, 68
Queen of Heaven Orphanage, 80

Randolph, Mary, 20
Ready, Martha A. (Mattie Silks), 68
Red Cross training school/Loretto
    Heights College, 96–97

Reed, Mary Dean (Mrs. Verner Z.), 6,
    14–16, 91–92
Retta Foote Memorial Organ/Colorado
    Women's College, 26
Revelle, Barbara Jo, 62–63
Reynolds, Cathy, 58
Reynolds, Minnie J., 40–41
Robert, Chaer, 58
Robinson, Cleo Parker, 20–21
Robinson, Helen Ring, 46
Roche, Josephine Aspenwall, 56–57
Rodgers, Mark, 90
Roeschlaub, Robert S., 34
Rogers, Jenny, 66, 68–69
Romer, Bea Miller (Mrs. Roy), 36
Ross, Gertie N. (Mrs. George), 16, 18, 20
Routt, Eliza Pickrell (Mrs. John L.), 48

Sabin, Dr. Florence Rena, 48, 56, 59
Sacred Heart School, 14
Salvation Army 4, 44
Schroeder, Patricia Scott, 62
Semple Brown Morris, 70
Shorter African Methodist Episcopal
    (A.M.E.) Church, 10, 20–21
Silks, Mattie, 66, 68–69
Sisters of Charity of Cincinnati, 14
Sisters of Loretto, 44–45, 96–97
Sisters of St. Benedict, 74
Sisters of the Sacred Heart, 80–81

Smedley House, Ninth Street Park/Auraria Campus, 72
Smith, Martha (Mrs. F. I.), 24
Smith, Mary E., 20
Social Center and Day Nursery, 14
South Side Woman's Club, 94
Speer, Kate A. (Mrs. Robert), 56
Speer, Robert—Mayor of Denver, 56
St. Cajetan's Catholic Church, 72, 74–75, 78
St. Cajetan's Center/Auraria Campus, 72, 74–75
St. Elizabeth's Catholic Church, 72, 74–75
St. Francis Interfaith Center/Auraria Campus, 74
St. Luke's Hospital School of Nursing, 32
St. Mary's Academy, 44–45, 96–97
St. Rose Residence for Women/St. Elizabeth's Catholic Church, 74
State Capitol, Colorado, 46–49, 101, 102
Statuary Hall, National Capitol, 56
Stepp, Geraldine, 7, 12
Sterner, Frederick J., 34
Stewart, Paul, 12
Stiles, Grace, 10
Stockton, Ruth Small, 48, 102
Sudler, James Associates, 54

Tabor, Augusta Pierce (Mrs. H. A. W.), 62–63
Tammen, Agnes Reid (Mrs. Harry H.), 6, 32
Teikyo Loretto Heights University, 96–97
Treat Hall/Colorado Women's College, 24–25
Trevorrow Hall, Lamont School of Music, 3, 92
Tri-State/Denver Buddhist Temple, 66–67
Truth, Sojourner, 30–31
Tryba, David Owen, 94

United Way, 28
Unity Church, 38, 62–63
University of Colorado at Denver, 72
University of Denver (DU), 3, 26, 52, 64, 90–93

Vanderhoof, Merrie Lynn (Mrs. John), 36
Varian and Varian, 40

Wales, Mary T., 26
Walker, A'Lelia, 10
Walker, Madam C. J., 10–11
Walsh, Sister Joanna, 44
Warren, Elizabeth Iliff (also Mrs. John Iliff, Mrs. Henry Warren), 90
Wayne, Frances "Pinkie," 60
Webb, Wellington—Mayor of Denver, 30, 58
Webb, Wilma J. (Mrs. Wellington), 30
Wells Fargo Bank Plaza, 62–63
Whatley Chapel/Colorado Women's College, 24, 26–27
Whatley, Gertrude (Mrs. Barney), 26
Wheatley, Phyllis, 16
White, Jr., Edward D., 36, 72, 88
Wieger, T. Robert, 28
Willard, Frances Elizabeth, 84
Willison, Robert, 72
Wolcott Arms Apartments, 34
Wolcott School for Girls, 34–35
Wolcott Vaile, Anna, 34
Wolfe Hall, 34
Woman's Christian Temperance Union (WCTU), 48–49, 84–85
Woman's Club of Denver (WCD), 38–39, 94
Woman's Club, South Side, 94–95
Women's Bank of Colorado, 64
Women's College/University of Denver, 26, 92
Women's Gold tapestry, 48
Women's History Month, 74
Women's Relief Corps, 48
Women's Wall/Denver Convention Center, 62–63
Wood, Leah J. (Jenny Rogers), 68
Working, Grace Booth, 88–89

Young Women's Christian Association (YWCA), 16–17